GAME
THINKING

Publishing Information

Copyright © 2018 gamethinking.io

Published by gamethinking.io,
315 Concord Way,
Burlingame CA 94010

ISBN 978-0-9997885-4-7

Second Edition

Production Credits

Illustrated by Scott Kim, with additional illustrations by Naida Jazmín Ochoa, Manny Aguiler

Editing and layout by Misha Gericke

Index by Jan Wright

GAME
THINKING

innovate smarter &
drive deep engagement
with design techniques
from hit games

Amy Jo Kim

Foreword by Raph Koster   Illustrated by Scott Kim

Table of Contents

Acknowledgements

I've been blessed with a wide circle of wonderful people who've helped bring these ideas to life.

My father, Wesley Bilson, is a serial entrepreneur who created new businesses in healthcare and renewable energy. My mother, Barbara Bilson-Woodruff, is a gifted and passionate educator who influenced a generation of students with her immersive, experiential Shakespeare classes. I'm proud to carry on this tradition of innovation in my Game Thinking work, where we combine coaching, education, and an entrepreneur's approach to product development.

Much of the credit for this book goes to my husband and partner in crime, Scott Kim, who created the visual design and illustrations, and shepherded the publishing process. This book would not be in your hands without Scott's brilliance and hard work.

Many thanks to our production team. Misha Gericke edited and laid out the book. Jan Wright did the indexing. Naida Jazmín Ochoa drew the charming cartoons of people scattered throughout the book. Manny Aguiler drew the 3d diagrams of the MVP canvas and social action matrix.

A special shout-out goes to Raph Koster, my long-time collaborator and friend, who wrote the beautiful preface. Raph has many creative gifts, but his first love was writing and it shows.

I'm deeply grateful to the colleagues, clients, and students who've helped me shape these far-ranging ideas into a tight, road-tested design framework. Thank you Ashita Achuthan, Paul Adams, Robin Allenson, Cindy Alvarez, Jeff Atwood, Irene Au, Cindy Au, Luc Bartholet, Jim Banister, Tomer Ben-Kiki, Buster Benson, Candis Best, Sair Buckle, Tim Chang, Jaxton Cheah, Dan Cook, Dennis Crowley, Nadya Direkova, Josh Elman, Blair Ethington, Laura Foley, Janice Fraser, Tracy Fullerton, Richard Garriott, Curtis Gilbert, Jeff Gothelf, Tom Gooden, Erika Hall, Steve Hoffman, Erin Hoffman-John, Chelsea Howe, Jason Hreha, Charles Hudson, Samuel Hulick, Tom Illmensee, Katherine Isbister, Mimi Ito, Naresh Jain, Vinayak Joglekar, Karl Kapp, Kevin Kelly, Donna Kelley, Laura Klein, Ranan Lachman, Felipe Lara, Matt Leacock, Ofer Leidner, Jeremy Liew, Kenneth Lim, Starr Long, Greg LoPiccolo, Megan Mahdavi, Wanda Meloni, Cara Meverden, David Mullich, David Murray, Dan Olsen, Myrian Pauillac, Jeff Patton, Steve Portigal, Sandie Richards, Eric Ries, Tracy Rosenthal-Newsom, Alex Rigopulos, Lisa Rutherford, Jesse Schell, Mike Sellers, Hiten Shah, Sarah Shewey, Michael Spiegelman, Jared Spool, Tony Stubblebine, Jeff Tseng, Steve Vassallo, Margaret Wallace. Casey Winters, Christina Wodtke, Will Wright, Robin Yang, and Eric Zimmerman. We couldn't have done it without you.

FREE BONUS

Get your free interactive MVP canvas
from the companion site for this book
gamethinkingbook.io
You will use this form in chapter 1
to help you hone your elevator
pitch, and to validate your
riskiest assumptions.

Foreword

by Raph Koster

Game designer, author of *A Theory of Fun*

Making stuff is hard.

We all know it. First, you aren't sure what to make, then you start making it and you're convinced it's right, then it's all wrong...and you go back and forth right up until the terrifying moment when you put it in front of someone else. And they hate it, or love it. Or worse, they are indifferent, that painful middle ground where you don't elicit any strong emotions at all. That's the moment when you sit back and wonder to yourself, "what could I have done differently?"

Amy Jo Kim has an answer for that, and it's this book. It's nothing less than *what you could have done differently*, laid out in concise, clear language, with diagrams, case studies, and processes.

I come from the world of games, and Amy Jo labels this approach "game thinking." (I could only wish that all of our projects used a process like what she describes here!) She calls it that because it is inspired by the way in which we game designers think of our players and their journeys: as a process of learning, guided by feedback, of hobby- and habit-building. A process of getting players to care.

In games, we don't have any utility to offer, you see. We just offer respite, enjoyment, a break from a busy day. We don't have *usefulness* on our side, unlike most products. We have to rely on the real fundamentals: why does a human like something? Why does a human return to something? Why do they *care*? We design to elicit that caring, that emotional attachment.

That's really what game thinking is about. It begins by pushing you to look at what your users actually care about, through its process of interviews and job stories. It asks you to listen—*really listen*—when users tell you what problems they have, and what solutions they wish were out there. It does away with hoary generalizations and made-up personas and goes right to the people most likely to want a solution from you, and teaches you, the designer, how to ask the right questions.

Then the book proceeds to guide you through the process of making that solution, in the right order, validating and confirming your premises along the way. Pushing you toward a design that's about the player growing, changing, and learning through use of your product.

In games, we almost take that for granted. We just know that someone who starts out in a game has a lot to learn and that, by the end, they will be jumping, twirling, dodging, building, and trading like crazy, juggling a dense panoply of systems and intricacies. So we design for it. We build that journey into the very shape of the product, with levels and learnings that unfold as the player reaches the right competencies. It's not easy, but we do it a lot, so much that we often don't even talk about it.

That may be why everyone seems to get what we do so wrong.

These days, when everybody sprinkles badges and points on top of everything, it may seem a little late to say "you've all missed the point!" Because game designers don't design badges and points systems. That's not the heart of what we do. We build systems that teach you themselves. We build systems that enable people to do things they didn't think they could do—whether it's drive a race car, score a goal in the World Cup, or blast an alien monster in the face. What we do is build systems that unveil possibility. Points and badges and the rest are just markers along the way, and never the goal.

Wouldn't it be nice if the systems, the products, the services we used today were about that? About unveiling possibility? Meeting needs? About putting the users before the bland and vague ideological mission, above the endless metrics? About enabling people to do what they didn't think they *could* do? About expanding what was possible?

It isn't only about what you, the designer, could be doing differently. It's about what your customers, your users, your clients, could be doing differently. It's about creating real value, not just using parasitic means of extracting revenue.

In the end, when we make games, we're working to bring more joy into the world. That's too big a task to be left only to us game folk. It should be part and parcel of every design. That's what game thinking can really mean. And that's what Amy Jo is documenting in this book: a method aimed at creating that core satisfaction a player feels when they turn to their partner and say "wow, that was *great*."

So here it is. What you can do differently, to make a real difference.

Introduction

What do the teams behind break-out products have in common? How can we follow in their footsteps?

This year, many innovative new products and services will launch, but only a handful will earn long-term success. Most will fail before they even get the chance.

Why is that? **What do the teams that produce break-out products have in common?** Can we follow in their footsteps, and reliably increase our odds of doing the same?

I say yes.

Let me take you back to a beautiful September day in Half Moon Bay, California. I was sitting in my living room, listening to the brilliant CEO of a hot gaming startup pitch me his idea for a social game where people with no musical talent would play plastic instruments and *feel* as if they were playing in a band. I joined the team—and that crazy idea turned into *Rock Band*, a genre-defining worldwide hit.

Later, I worked on *The Sims* with Will Wright, a visionary game designer with some unorthodox methods for unlocking creativity. That project almost got cancelled a few weeks before shipping—and then went on to become the biggest-selling PC game franchise of all time.

A few years after that, I worked on *Covet Fashion*, an innovative mobile game that incorporates high-fashion clothing from real-world brands. What we built was different than our original idea—and we weren't sure how it would work out.

That game became an evergreen hit franchise that enables millions of players to create fabulous outfits from designer collections, and even purchase those clothes in real life.

Lessons from Gaming

How do hit games grab people's attention and keep them coming back? What makes an experience truly engaging over time?

I've worked on massive hit games that reached millions of people. Yet none of these games appeals to everyone. Stylistically, people seek out a wide variety of experiences. While I enjoy *Rock Band* and *Covet Fashion*, my son prefers adrenaline-pumping shooters and my best friend is addicted to candy-coated puzzlers.

One person's beloved game is another's worst nightmare.

Setup the Conditions for Flow.

Successful games all have something in common: *the intrinsic joy of skill-building*. It feels good to engage our brains, improve our skills, and make progress along a path toward mastery. Games, sports, and education are particularly good at laying out this path—but every product leader can learn to harness the underlying power of skill-building and challenge.

Structured activities like games, sports, office work, and fund-raising all revolve around developing and using a skill. **If the level of challenge increases to match your evolving skill, you've got a setup for flow**—the ultimate goal of every game and product designer.

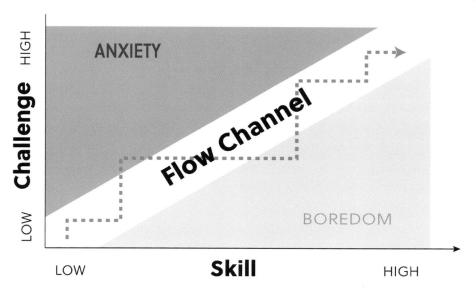

Flow is not about making things easy, or "gamified." Flow takes effort. **Without learning, practice, and challenge, there is no flow.** At their core, games are pleasurable learning engines that deliver an experience that's deeply, intrinsically motivating. Over time, you absorb the rules, build your skills, tackle ever-greater challenges—and in the process, you're transformed in some way that's meaningful to YOU.

Forget Points, Think Character Transformation.

Just as character transformation is the backbone of great drama, **personal transformation is the backbone of great gameplay**. In games, *we* are the protagonist—the person with agency, facing a series of choices and challenges along our journey towards mastery.

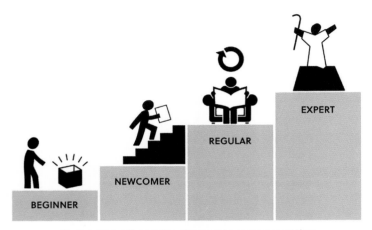

Personal transformation drives engagement over time

Progress metrics like points, badges, levels, leaderboards, and reputation systems are icing on this learning/mastery cake. These markers help you gauge where you stand, and how far you've come—but they're meaningless as a stand-alone system without something to master. If you want to build a compelling product experience, forget points—think character transformation.

Blend Intrinsic Pleasure with Extrinsic Scaffolding.

Games are built from systems and rules that engage you in a micro-world, a "magic circle" that's shared by everyone playing the game. In a magic circle, ordinary activities take on special meaning—throwing a ball into a net becomes scoring a goal.

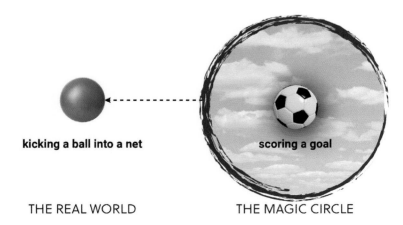

kicking a ball into a net   scoring a goal

THE REAL WORLD   THE MAGIC CIRCLE

Well-crafted games are an artful blend of intrinsic pleasure and extrinsic scaffolding. They invite you to take a mini-break from daily life, and spend time (together) in an alternate, simplified reality. Pleasurable activities are the beating heart of this micro-world, and progress scaffolding (points, levels, badges, power-ups) serves to support and amplify these core activities.

The Trinity of Intrinsic Motivation

To create a truly compelling experience, tap into the trinity of Intrinsic Motivation: Autonomy, Mastery, and Purpose. This framework emerged during the 1970s as **self-determination theory**, and was re-popularized in Dan Pink's book, *Drive*, on workplace motivation.

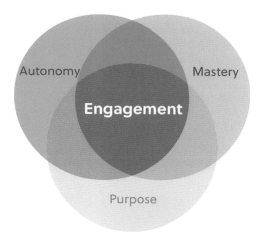

To avoid the trap of short-term engagement, use these three universal drives as a starting point when you're designing feedback and rewards for your experience. We'll cover that in Section III: Design.

I'll refer to these intrinsic drives throughout this Handbook—look for the Trinity symbol to guide your way.

Autonomy: Self-Determination and Meaningful Choice

Autonomy is the feeling of controlling your own destiny. In a game, app, or service. This boils down to how and when you offer choices. Great games offer meaningful choices with interesting constraints. Think of *Settlers of Catan*, *World of Warcraft*, *Minecraft*, even Kickstarter—all systems that can be explored and mastered by following your interests and making a series of increasingly interesting choices.

Mastery: Skill-Building, Feedback and Challenge

Mastery taps into the feeling of getting better at something. Games offer the player a set of actions and choices within a constrained, rule-based environment. In a great game, mastering the rule-set is deeply pleasurable. The lack of anything to master is often why simple gamification fails. Points, badges, and leaderboards aren't compelling unless you're improving along some personally meaningful dimension.

Purpose: Connect with Something Greater than Yourself

Purpose is about connectedness and relatedness—with other people, with a shared cause, with something bigger than yourself. Numerous studies show us that people who cultivate meaningful relationships report higher levels of happiness. Purpose is often communicated through storytelling—and you know what? **The most powerful story is happening inside your customer's head**, a personal narrative of how engaging with your product will transform them into a more powerful, more skillful, more connected version of themselves.

Game Design ≠ Loyalty Marketing

Digging into intrinsic motivation will help you design compelling experiences and avoid some common pitfalls of gamification. Progress metrics like points, badges, and levels are easy to see and tempting to use. But that's not where the magic is.

People who come from a marketing background look at games and see a set of extrinsic motivators and reward schedules that can be lifted out and plunked down elsewhere. That's understandable, as because points, levels, status, and rewards are the atomic units of loyalty programs, a staple in the marketer's playbook.

Although loyalty programs are superficially similar to games, they look very different when viewed through the lens of intrinsic motivation. **Trying to drive long-term engagement with extrinsic rewards is a fool's errand.** If metrics and rewards are your main event, you've got a shallow and/or manipulative product that won't hold people's interest over time. Even worse, you might be dampening their creativity and enthusiasm without knowing it.

Extrinsic Rewards Can Devalue Pleasurable Activities

In his book on workplace motivation, Dan Pink summarizes three decades of research into one compelling punchline: **Extrinsic rewards are effective at getting people to complete simple, short-term tasks, but** *decrease* **effectiveness for creative tasks that require out-of-the-box thinking.**

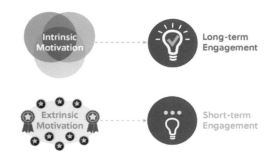

Numerous studies show that extrinsic rewards can devalue otherwise pleasurable tasks like reading or drawing. For example, in one study, kids who loved reading were rewarded with points and money for completing chapters. Guess what happened? The kids completely stopped reading for pleasure. Unintended side-effects can be brutal. It's easier than you think to kill off intrinsic motivation with external rewards.

From Game Design to Product Design

The principles behind game thinking led to such breakthrough hit games as *Rock Band*, *The Sims*, and *Covet Fashion*. But if you're building a product, don't worry. These same principles led to products and services like Slack, Kickstarter, and Happify.

Game thinking puts the skill-building power of games into the hands of product leaders. After helping innovative hits like *Rock Band*, *The Sims*, and *Covet Fashion* come to life, I now work with entrepreneurs worldwide, helping them use game thinking to innovate faster and smarter.

Entrepreneurs like Megan Mahdavi, CEO of Sunreach, who used game thinking to validate her idea for leveraging young talent in developing countries. While working a full-time job, Megan tested her idea and got some disheartening early feedback from her intended customers. Digging deeper, she found an adjacent high-need group who appreciated and embraced her model. Armed with this early validation, Megan quit her job and now runs a successful, high-growth SAAS consulting company that trains young people in Haiti and Palestine to become Salesforce engineers.

Game thinking also helped Ofer Leidner and Tomer Ben-kiki, serial entrepreneurs who'd sold a casual gaming company and were ready for their next challenge. They'd developed a game idea around the science of happiness, which we tested with several groups of high-need customers. We found a pocket of superfans to help in tune our early systems. Happify is now the market leader in mental health and well-being services.

Then there's Ranan Lachman, CEO of Pley. Ranan and his team utilized game thinking to validate their idea for a community extension to their fast-growing toy rental service. We discovered that Pley customers wanted educational video content, so we built an MVP video community and avoided spending resources on what people didn't want.

Embrace and Extend: Lean Startup and Design Thinking

Through these experiences, I've learned first-hand that **the same thing which makes a game successful can also make a product successful: your product.**

In this book, I will walk you through the steps of game thinking—a process you can use to validate and develop your product idea.

Game thinking embraces and extends existing product development methods.

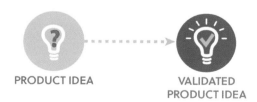

PRODUCT IDEA   VALIDATED PRODUCT IDEA

If you're a fan of **lean/agile** methods, you know how to refine and test your idea using the build-measure-learn cycle.

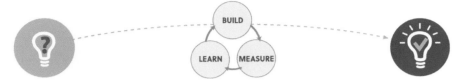

If you're familiar with **design thinking**, you know how to empathize with customers, and use what you learn to prototype solutions that fill real customer needs.

What game thinking adds to these methods is an innovation framework for finding early hot-core customers, and taking them on a journey toward mastery.

The best products don't just fill a need. They help people get better at something they care about.

Game thinking is a framework for building products that make your customers more powerful, knowledgeable, and connected. Like lean startup, game thinking is grounded in testing assumptions. And like design thinking, we start out in a problem space (an unmet need) and end in a solution space (how your product fills that need).

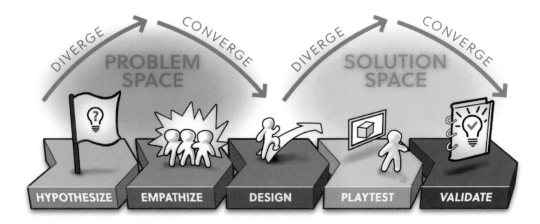

5 Steps to Product/Market Fit

The five sections of this book cover the five steps of the game thinking process.

Step 1. Hypothesize
Run smarter experiments by clarifying your product idea and identifying your high-risk assumptions.

Step 2. Empathize
Find hot-core early customers who are passionate about your product idea and can help you test your assumptions.

Step 3. Design
Map out a path to mastery and learning architecture that takes your customers from beginner to expert.

Step 4. Playtest
Prototype your ideas using Superfan insights, then run high-learning playtests to validate your assumptions.

Step 5. Reflect
Summarize what you learned, how you learned it, and what you plan to do next based on your data.

What You'll Learn

Here are three things you'll learn in this book and will be able to apply to your own projects right away.

1. What role game thinking plays in designing hit products.

2. How applying game thinking methods to your product will help you build long-term engagement and increase your odds of success.

3. How the game thinking tool kit—a proven step-by-step system—can help you get reliably better outcomes from your innovation efforts.

To start, we need to go back to the beginning, because that's where good results are.

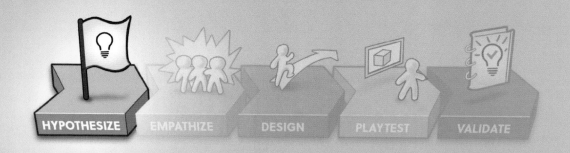

HYPOTHESIZE EMPATHIZE DESIGN PLAYTEST VALIDATE

SECTION I
Hypothesize

The best way to have a good idea is to have lots of ideas.
Linus Pauling, Scientist

You've got an idea for a new product—something you're excited about. How do you validate your idea and find success? The answer is simple, yet paradoxical: **success comes from combining a strong vision with a relentless search for the truth.** If your efforts aren't grounded in vision and purpose, you're shooting in the dark.

But vision alone isn't enough. To build a successful product, **your hunger for market feedback must override your ego.** The innovators who create breakthrough products are relentless about **shaping vision through iterative testing**. They hypothesize about what could be—and gather data to refine their thinking and satisfy their search for market validation.

In this section, you'll learn how to run smarter product experiments by emulating these success stories and creating testable hypotheses about your product, customers, and market conditions.

Chapter 1

Clarify Your Product Strategy

To increase your chances of success, minimize your time through the build-measure-learn cycle.

Eric Ries, Author, *The Lean Startup*

To TURN A PROMISING IDEA into a successful product, it's important to start at the beginning and run experiments that are grounded in clear, testable hypotheses. But how do you generate those hypotheses? And how do you prioritize which ones to test?

Many entrepreneurs will just start building whatever they think might be interesting. Some use the Business Model Canvas (or something similar) to get started (a "canvas" is a one-page worksheet you complete to capture at-a-glance insights and goals). While this helps you think through your whole business, it doesn't help you focus on the most pressing issues involved in testing and validating an idea and building your MVP (minimum viable product).

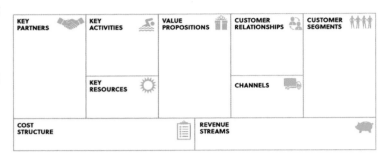

Meet the MVP Canvas

To help you develop strong, testable hypotheses and run smarter experiments, I've created a stripped-down tool called the MVP Canvas that helps you **frame your current ideas as hypotheses, and generate prioritized assumptions to test**. If you've ever wanted a reliable way to validate ideas quickly, this tool is for you.

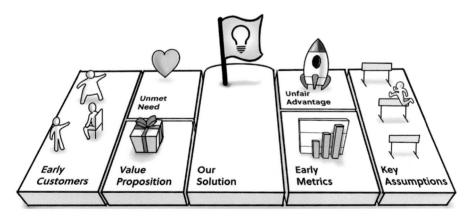

Focus on Early Customers and Unmet Needs

Successful innovations may end up reaching a mainstream audience—but they never start off that way. That's the paradox of innovation: **the "typical" people in your market are not the same ones you need to delight when bringing your idea to life.**

Innovation Diffusion Theory and Crossing the Chasm

Back in 1961, Everett Rogers described this dynamic in his seminal theory, *Diffusion of Innovations*. Rogers identified five distinct groups of people who engage with new innovations over time:**Innovators:** eager to try out and mess around with daring or risky new ideas.

- **Early Adopters:** driven by need to solve a pressing problem—willing to take risk and put up with a messy or incomplete solution to get the core value.

- **Early Majority:** interested in the solution, willing to adopt only when seeing social proof. Can be transformed if pain point becomes pressing.

- **Late Majority:** risk-averse, resource-constrained; waits for social pressure to adopt.

- **Laggards:** looks to the past—averse to the new; don't perceive a need to adopt.

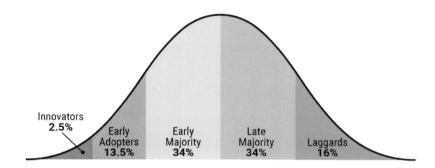

Years later, Geoffrey Moore popularized and expanded on Roger's model in *Crossing the Chasm*. In this popular marketing book, Moore weaves a compelling story about how he turned the Apple II hobbyist computer into a mainstream consumer hit—and "crossed the chasm" into mainstream success by transitioning from early adopters to early majority.

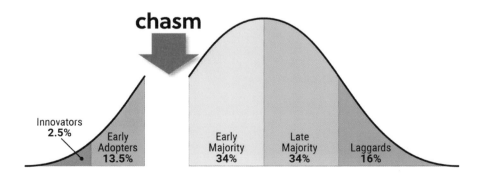

Here's the punchline: **if you're innovating, you need to find and delight a small early market before you target that larger segment.** Your odds of succeeding go WAY up when you test your idea with a small group of people who need what you're offering, and will **put up with cost, ridicule, and friction to get those needs met**.

Finding these high-need, high-value early customers is an iterative process that you can accelerate by writing down clear, testable hypotheses. Ask yourself: *What group of people will need and want our offering first? What characteristics and behaviors will they have in common?*

The best way to develop loyal customers is to fulfill their needs in a pleasurable way. Think about the customers you're targeting and ask yourself: *What relevant needs do they have right now that we could potentially address? How are they currently getting those needs met? Why is that unsatisfying?*

Don't worry about getting it right. Just jot down your current thinking. Your job is to make educated guesses and turning those into hypotheses you can test.

Developing a New Product

Let's bring this to life by looking at how Happify, a successful mental health app, created and tested their early customer hypotheses. At the start, we had three hypotheses about who would most need a game that promotes science-based happiness—and what their unmet need might be. We put those into the MVP Canvas.

Group 1: Hard-driving entrepreneurs (like ourselves) with a lot of situational stress
Unmet Need: convenient and effective stress management

Group 2: Professionals recently diagnosed with depression
Unmet Need: an alternative (or supplement) to psychiatric drugs

Group 3: People going through a major life change, e.g. divorce, kids, empty nest
Unmet Need: help with adjusting to a "new normal" and keeping the blues at bay

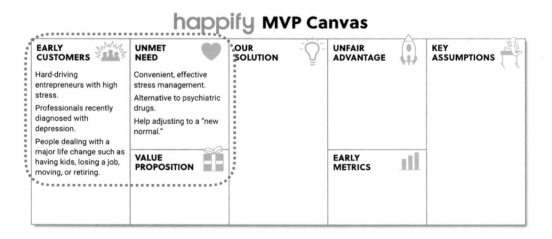

Chelsea Howe on Beginner Mistakes

Chelsea Howe is a game designer, community organizer of local game jams, creative director, and champion of underdogs and outsiders everywhere.

I love watching first-time designers make games. They bite off way more than they can chew.

Beginners start off with an idea, then change it, and change it again. They don't have a consistent hypothesis, so they fall prey to feature creep.

It's hard for beginners to throw out work—they see that as wasted effort, rather than valuing learning. It's silly to assume that 100% of what's created will make it to launch. You need to see failure is part of an iterative process.

Once we generated these hypotheses, we ran early experiments to figure out which group to focus on—and what product to build for them. You'll learn about how that played out in the following chapters.

Developing a Major New Feature or Product Extension

You can also use this approach to validate new features for an existing product. For example, we helped Pley validate their idea for a major product extension: a customer community where Lego-loving parents could chat about their beloved hobby. Pley had thousands of existing customers, many with strong opinions about which features they wanted to see added to the service. The question was: who did we need to listen to and focus on?

To select the right customers for our experiments, we thought about which subscribers would be likely to participate in an online community and came up with a metric:

Test Subjects: subscribers who upload photos and videos of their kids' Lego creations
Unmet Need: a place to chat with other Pley parents about their favorite hobby

In this situation, we didn't need to generate multiple hypotheses, because we found a promising group of people to test our idea on by data-mining an existing list. Sometimes, that's the right way to get started. Here's how the canvas looks so far.

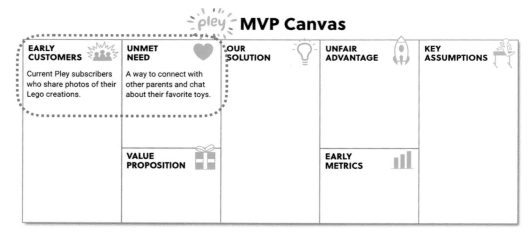

In the next few chapters, you'll find out what we learned from our Pley research, and how those insights resulted in a major pivot for the development team.

Connect Your Solution to Customer Value

Many entrepreneurs, myself included, get attached to their solution before considering how it solves an existing problem for specific people. Here's a harsh truth: **People don't care about your solution, they care about finding the easiest, most convenient, most effective way to meet their needs.**

Your solution is a hypothesis—not a given. When you start with delivering customer value, you realize there may be many possible solutions to your customer's problem—not just the one you have in mind.

To make this connection, write down a brief, high-level description of your solution hypothesis, i.e. your elevator pitch. Connect that to your Value Proposition by asking yourself:

- How does my solution address my customer's unmet needs?

- From their point of view, what unique value proposition are we offering?

- What makes our solution different from everything else out there?

Customer Value Connects to Unmet Need

You might have trouble differentiating between customer value proposition and unmet need. That's because they're closely related. Customer needs exist in problem space— whether or not your project is in the mix. Your value proposition exists in solution space— it's the connective tissue between your solution and your customer's needs.

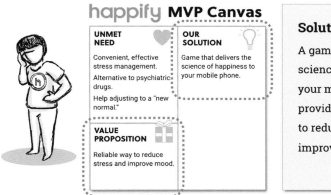

happify MVP Canvas

UNMET NEED
Convenient, effective stress management.
Alternative to psychiatric drugs.
Help adjusting to a "new normal."

OUR SOLUTION
Game that delivers the science of happiness to your mobile phone.

VALUE PROPOSITION
Reliable way to reduce stress and improve mood.

Solution/Value Pair

A game that delivers the science of happiness to your mobile phone, and provides a reliable way to reduce stress and improve mood.

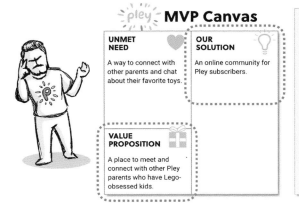

pley MVP Canvas

UNMET NEED
A way to connect with other parents and chat about their favorite toys.

OUR SOLUTION
An online community for Pley subscribers.

VALUE PROPOSITION
A place to meet and connect with other Pley parents who have Lego-obsessed kids.

Solution/Value Pair

An online community for our subscribers, to connect them with other parents who have creative, Lego-obsessed kids.

Define Your Unfair Advantage and Early Metrics

Next, you're going to write down your unfair advantage—the special skills, resources, connections and knowledge that makes you and your team the right people to bring this idea to life.

Stating this up-front—and keeping it in mind when analyzing your research—will help you stay focused on your vision and passion, amidst all the customer feedback.

Hedgehog Concept

To identify your unfair advantage, get inspired by the "hedgehog concept" from *Good to Great* by Jim Collins. Ask yourself: ***What am I passionate about? What are we the best in the world at? Why should someone believe in this team and project?***

Companies that build lasting value have good answers to those questions. Combine that with a strong economic engine and you're on the path to success.

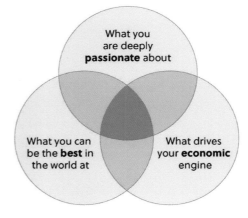

Early Metrics

You can't change what you can't measure. When you're doing subjective research with early adopters, you don't have enough data for A/B tests, so choose a subjective metric connected to your product goals. Jot down one or two relevant factors you can measure in upcoming experiments, such as:

- Preference: old vs new (for a redesign)

- Uptake: willingness to use the product

- Value: willingness to pay for the product

- NPS score: willingness to recommend it to other people

Christina Wodtke on Design Thinking

Christina Wodtke is a designer, educator and author who's worked for Yahoo, LinkedIn, Myspace, and Zynga. She now teaches UX and design thinking at Stanford University.

When I first heard about design thinking, I thought it was a load of hooey. I thought someone was just rebranding User-Centered Design as something they could sell for more money.

Then, I was invited to teach at the Copenhagen Institute for Interaction Design. I took those students through a one-week version of my entrepreneurship class and they got to product/market fit in one week. That really shook me up—how could they get to product/market fit so quickly!?

I realized that it was because they used design thinking at every step—the way they talked to people, managed data, prototyped, and tested. When I came back home, I put design thinking into my classes.

Startups don't have much time, so you've got to grab anything that makes you faster and more effective, and hold on tight.

For Happify, our unfair advantage was the team's experience with running and selling a successful casual games company, and a personal passion for bringing the science of happiness to a wider audience. Our early metrics were built around getting positive reactions to our prototype.

For Pley, our unfair advantage was a fast-growing service with a strong internal development team. Our business goals centered around decreasing subscriber churn, so we agreed to look for solutions that would achieve that end.

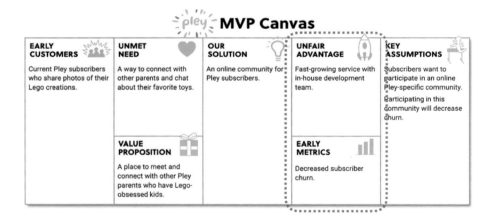

Prioritize Your Assumptions

Now it's time to articulate and prioritize your assumptions.

To generate this list, look through the hypotheses you've written down so far in the MVP Canvas. Ask yourself: which assumptions am I least sure about? Which ones would devastate my project if they turned out to be false?

Your goal is to write down a prioritized list of your high-risk assumptions—the ones central to your project that you're unsure about. Pay special attention to the left side of your Canvas. Who are your assumptions' early customers and what are their unmet needs? What about your solution and value prop?

This list will help you get the most out of your customer research, so make the assumptions concrete and testable. Write down things that seem obvious, but need confirmation. Then identify the most crucial, bet-the-company assumptions on this list. Which ones could sink your entire project or company? Which ones make you feel nervous? Those are the ones you need to focus on.

Get Ready to Run Your High-Learning Experiments

Now that you understand how to fill out your MVP Canvas and prioritize your assumptions, you're on your way to running high-learning experiments and creating a compelling product from the ground up.

In the next chapter, you'll learn how to use this analysis to plan your product discovery research and set yourself up for success.

Worksheet: MVP Canvas

Now it's your turn. Answer these questions to fill out your MVP canvas. If you're testing several different hypotheses, you may want to fill out more than one canvas.

> ⬇ Download a free interactive version of the MVP canvas from the book companion site **gamethinkingbook.io**

Articulate Your Product/Customer Hypothesis

Who will be your first 25–50 passionate early customers?

_____

_____

_____

What unmet need will your product meet and fulfill?

_____

_____

_____

What's your solution that meets this need for these people?

_____

_____

_____

What value proposition connects your solution to your early customers' unmet needs?

_____

_____

_____

Identify Your Key Strengths and Early Metrics

Why you? Why this team? What are your key strengths? What's your unfair advantage (your sweet spot/secret sauce)?

_____

_____

_____

What early metrics will you use to measure success—and why?

_____

_____

_____

Prioritize Your Highest-Risk Assumptions

Which assumptions about your project do you most need to test, and why? Which ones would spell DISASTER if they turned out to be false?

_____

_____

_____

Draft Your Elevator Pitch

We are developing...

_____

_____

...for...

_____

...so they can...

_____

_____

Product Strategy Speed Bumps

When MVP experiments fail, it's often due to well-meaning people lacking an understanding of the nature of early product development. Watch out for these speed bumps along your path as you build and develop your MVP.

Speed bump #1: The mass market visionary

Teams that stumble often do so because they go broad first, skipping the crucial stage of finding and delighting their early customers. These teams are often led by mass market visionaries—brilliant people who see where their product is headed, and what it could be, but not where it is right now. They're uncomfortable with focusing on a small early market of customers who fall outside their big vision of a mass-market product. The problem is, you won't get the chance to worry about a mass market if you fail to capture and delight your early market with your innovation.

If you're building something innovative, mainstream users will neither understand your creation nor give you the feedback you need to evolve. Instead, **find and delight a few high-need, high-value early customers.**

Speed bump #2: The passionate believer

It takes superhuman self-control to listen dispassionately while early customers rip your ideas apart. Consider a recent founder I worked with. He was eager to conduct early customer interviews and sure that he'd be an impartial interviewer, but during those sessions, his entrepreneurial passion took over. He just couldn't resist asking leading questions about the product and trying to talk people out of their reactions. To counteract this natural tendency, we trained a more junior person to conduct the interviews and used the entrepreneur's oversight and guidance to refine the interview script and lead the data analysis. This allowed us to get the honest feedback we needed to shape the product into a service that has thousands of paying subscribers today.

Avoid falling too deeply in love with the particulars of your idea. Instead, **test and refine the ideas with early adopters and a dispassionate interviewer.**

Speed bump #3: The data snob

Some people worship at the altar of analytics and believe that actionable research always involves A/B testing and thousands of data points. That's great if you're optimizing an existing product, but not useful if you're bringing something innovative to life. (Besides that, a product that is yet to be built has no users on which to run A/B tests.)

Data snobs set themselves up as the champions of the truth and dismiss any qualitative research as "unscientific." For example, while working once with a fast-growing startup on a website redesign, we mocked up and tested several variations on the core functionality, found a winning design that met our business goals and got high ratings from early customers. But then a project manager with an agenda dismissed our prototyping results as "too small to count." That company now has a rebranded website with a new logo and colors, but the same layout and functionality. No business problems were solved.

Use subjective tests to validate your early ideas. Innovation comes from early prototyping. Analytics come later. Know when to use both.

Speed bump #4: The high-gloss champion

High-gloss champions have a hard time with imagining how sketches and wireframes might evolve into something wonderful. Polished visuals can fool them into thinking something is further along than it is.

Visual quality is important for a finished product. Nobody wants to ship something that is ugly and hard to use. For early discovery, however, polished visuals can be a major speed bump. Take my former client, a brilliant young CEO who came to me with gorgeous mock-ups that he believed were "close to final product" (they were not). He insisted on seeing that level of polish in everything we showed to early customers, and our progress slowed to a crawl. Even worse, the team became attached to the beautiful visuals we'd crafted, so when we discovered problems with the core value proposition, the team resisted those results and the product ultimately failed.

Polished visuals are harder to change, both technically and emotionally. **For rapid iteration, keep your visuals pared down and simple.**

Chapter 2

Draft Your Product Brief

There is nothing quite so useless as doing with great efficiency something that should not be done at all.

Peter Drucker

IN CHAPTER 1, YOU LEARNED how to clarify your product strategy and articulate your key assumptions. Assumption-testing is embedded in the lean startup model, and frankly, it's one of the most difficult tasks you'll face.

It's natural to think your product idea is fantastic, something people will love. It's so much harder to challenge that belief, and eagerly look for what's wrong with your idea—as well as what's right with it.

The best way to counteract this natural tendency is to embrace uncertainty and create alternative hypotheses for what you might build. If you develop and test several different but related ideas, it's easier to be unattached to any particular outcome, and surface the best ones.

Stage-Gate Model of Innovation

There's a well-established theory of product innovation called the stage-gate model that can help us understand how this works. This model was popularized in 1986 by Robert Cooper in his book, *Winning at New Products*. It lays out a series of development stages, punctuated by decision-making "gates" that let the winning ideas pass through.

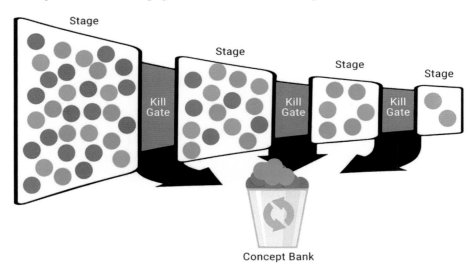

Concept Bank

In the early stages of your project, your goal is to test many small ideas, and continue developing the ones that "earned" their resources by making it through the gate. As you move along you develop fewer, bigger ideas—and eventually ship a single, coherent product.

The most successful game studios and tech startups I've worked with follow a version of this process. It's a guiding force behind game thinking—and a powerful way for you to embrace the search for truth and increase your odds of success.

What Is a Product Brief?

A key to smart planning is to start at the end and work backwards. Following that principle, I'm now going to show you how to create a draft product brief. This document tells the story of what your product is, who it's for, and how you'll test your ideas. It has three sections:

> **Section 1) Product Strategy:** What We're Building
>
> **Section 2) Customer Insights:** What We're Learning
>
> **Section 3) Pivot or Persevere:** What to Build Next

Drafting this document early, before you have all the answers, is a great way to refine your current thinking and formulate a smart and efficient testing plan. As you test your assumptions, you'll update your product brief to reflect what you've learned and outline next steps (see Chapter 11). This will help you coordinate your efforts and communicate your vision to stakeholders, contractors, and colleagues.

Product Strategy: What We're Building

In the first section of your brief, you'll outline your current product strategy—knowing that you'll update this after you test your ideas with early customers.

Craft Your Elevator Pitch

You'll start with an elevator pitch—a clear, concise statement of what you want to create, who it's for, and why it's valuable to them.

Your pitch should be short enough to communicate in the time it takes to ride an elevator, and highlight the core value proposition for the intended audience, as simply and clearly as possible.

Use the Elevator Pitch Template below to tell the world what you're delivering, who it's for, and what customer problem or need you're addressing.

Elevator Pitch

We are building [your product concept in a nutshell]

for [your high-need, hot-core customers]

so they can [scratch an itch, fulfill a desire, target a pain point]

Your elevator pitch as a set of testable assumptions about your product, market, and team. Soon, you'll be testing and refining these assumptions with early adopters—so don't worry about "getting it right" at this stage, just write down your current thinking.

Include Your "Before" MVP Canvas

You'll also include your initial MVP canvas in this section (see Chapter 1). This has more details about your product and customer hypotheses, and the list of prioritized assumptions you're planning to test. Use your answers use as guidance when you're writing your elevator pitch—these two documents should echo each other.

After you test your ideas with early adopters, you'll update both your canvas and pitch to reflect what's changed, and what you learned.

BEFORE **MVP Canvas**

EARLY CUSTOMERS	UNMET NEED	OUR SOLUTION	UNFAIR ADVANTAGE	KEY ASSUMPTIONS
Not your ultimate larger audience, but who you will contact, design for, and sell to first.	Why do customers need your product? What problem does it solve?	What is your solution? How does this solve the customer's problem?	How is your company uniquely well suited to win?	What high-risk assumptions will you be testing as you build your MVP?

VALUE PROPOSITION	EARLY METRICS
Why will customers prefer your product over competing products? What's different and high-value?	What will you measure to determine if your early prototyping efforts are successful?

Customer Insights: What We're Learning

In this section, you'll summarize how you'll test your hypotheses, and what kind of insights you expect to gather.

Meet the Superfan Funnel

In game thinking, we use a three-stage process called the superfan funnel to accelerate product/market fit. In the following chapters, you'll learn in detail how this funnel works, and how to apply these powerful techniques to your own project.

Since you haven't done the research yet, you'll use this opportunity to sketch out a research plan that fits your project needs, and start thinking about how you'll identify and empathize with your early customers.

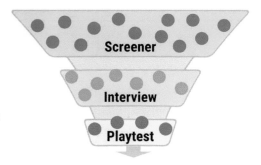

Dan Cook on Stage Gate Theory

Dan Cook is lead game designer and co-founder of
indie game studio Spry Fox, and writes the renowned
Lost Garden game design blog.

*One of the early lessons I learned about the game
industry is that failure is very, very likely. Even if you
execute wonderfully, there's only a small chance that your
dream idea will work out.*

*To improve my chances of success I use a popular
product development model called Stage Gate. Imagine a
funnel. At the top are a whole bunch of tiny little
experiments in the early concept stage.*

*Then there's a gate. The gate asks questions like: Is this
game prototype engaging for at least 15 minutes? Is our
rate of progress on improving the fun of this game fast
enough?*

*During the stage, you develop several concepts. During
the gate, you kill the weak ones, and move the rest on to
the next stage. Then you kill a bunch of those. You keep
doing this until you have one or two concepts you release
into the world.*

Planning Your Research: Who, What, When, Where

Look over your early market hypotheses from your MVP Canvas and ask yourself:

- Who will we bring in first for testing? How will we find them?

- Which assumptions will we be testing first? Why?

- Can we start right away, or is there a "gating event" for getting started?

- Will we talk to people online, by phone, or in person? Or a mix?

Research plan

WHO: [XX] people with [YY] characteristics.

WHAT: early interviews or playtests designed to test [Assumption 1]

WHEN: [XX] days from gating event.

WHERE: [geographic location: online, in-person, etc.]

WHY: tune our core systems, get early feedback on our direction.

Your answers will of course depend on the details of your project and customers. Here are the research plan summaries we wrote for Happify and Pley, along with their MVP Canvas answers.

We started each project with short interviews designed to test our core product idea and refine our understanding of unmet customer needs (see Chapter 4).

---

happify Research plan

WHO: parents with young kids who recently left the workforce.

WHAT: interviews designed to test their need for a happiness game.

WHEN: once we've identified potential subjects (no gating event).

WHERE: online, using either cellphone or Skype.

WHY: test our overall direction and target customer assumptions.

---

happify **MVP Canvas**

EARLY CUSTOMERS	UNMET NEED	OUR SOLUTION	UNFAIR ADVANTAGE	KEY ASSUMPTIONS
Hard-driving entrepreneurs with high stress. Professionals recently diagnosed with depression. People dealing with a major life change such as having kids, losing a job, moving, or retiring.	Convenient, effective stress management. Alternative to psychiatric drugs. Help adjusting to a "new normal."	Game that delivers the science of happiness to your mobile phone.	Experience running and selling a game company. Personal passion for the subject area.	People want a mobile solution to their mood challenges. People are willing to pay for this solution (vs. free alternatives). We can deliver a game that measurably changes your happiness levels.
	VALUE PROPOSITION Reliable way to reduce stress and improve mood.		**EARLY METRICS** Reaction to our first prototype: positive or negative.	

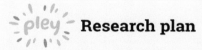 **Research plan**

WHO: subscribers with young kids who love playing with Legos.

WHAT: interviews meant to test their need for a Pley community.

WHEN: once we've identified potential subjects (no gating event).

WHERE: online, using either cellphone or Skype.

WHY: validate our product idea and value proposition.

pley **MVP Canvas**

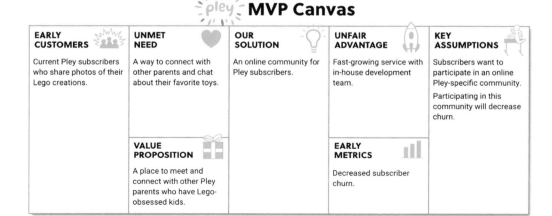

EARLY CUSTOMERS	UNMET NEED	OUR SOLUTION	UNFAIR ADVANTAGE	KEY ASSUMPTIONS
Current Pley subscribers who share photos of their Lego creations.	A way to connect with other parents and chat about their favorite toys.	An online community for Pley subscribers.	Fast-growing service with in-house development team.	Subscribers want to participate in an online Pley-specific community. Participating in this community will decrease churn.
	VALUE PROPOSITION A place to meet and connect with other Pley parents who have Lego-obsessed kids.		**EARLY METRICS** Decreased subscriber churn.	

Notice how the research plans are connected to that project's MVP Canvas? Make sure you connect your own research plan to your hypotheses about early customers and unmet needs—and also to the high-risk assumptions you want to test first.

Key Results and Observed Patterns

After you've tested your assumptions, you'll summarize your findings and highlight the most relevant, actionable results. Then you'll use those insights to update your product strategy and design, and decide what to do next.

For now, look at the research plan you just sketched out and imagine what kind of patterns or insights MIGHT arise out of your discussions with early customers. Given the assumptions you'll be testing, what kind of habits, needs, and new ideas are you expecting to hear about?

Here are some sample patterns to get your started. Gather your team for a brainstorming session, apply these to your project, and see what you come up with.

- **Pattern Template 1:** Many of our subjects like to <daily habit>.

- **Pattern Template 2:** Some of our subjects think that <idea or belief>.

- **Pattern Template 3:** The men we spoke with wish they could <unmet need>.

- **Pattern Template 4:** Few of our subjects are willing to pay for <your service>.

- **Pattern Template 5:** Most of our subjects tried out <your main competitor>.

As with everything in your product brief, these are hypotheses you'll test and refine over the next few weeks. If you already have insights or hunches about your hot-core customers, go ahead and add them to this list of hypotheses. This will help you get into your customer's mindset and focus your research.

Katherine Isbister on Research

Katherine Isbister runs the Center for Games and Playable Media at UC Santa Cruz, and is the author of *How Games Move Us: Emotion by Design.*

When a student has an idea, I always say "Show me other things in the landscape of this idea. How is your idea different from everything else out there? How is your idea better?" That's an important step that a lot of novice designers don't take.

I also have them spend time where the kinds of people they want to design for hang out. For example, if you want to design a casual game to be played on the subway, then ride the subway, and surreptitiously watch people playing on their phones. Do they switch tasks? How are people around them relating to them?

Notice what's going on in the situation, and integrate those insights into your game.

Here are some assumption-based hypotheses we generated for Happify and Pley.

happify Patterns

PATTERN 1: they love this idea, but aren't sure it'll work for them .

PATTERN 2: they want our game to look and feel like [X]

(some game or product they're already familiar with).

PATTERN 3: they're interested in the game, but wouldn't pay for it.

pley Patterns

PATTERN 1: they already participate in multiple online communities.

PATTERN 2: they want to meet other parents with similar interests.

PATTERN 3: they want better features for sharing photos & videos.

After playtesting, we updated these to distill what we'd learned (see Chapter 11).

Pivot or Persevere: What to Build Next

The third section of your product brief outlines what you plan to do next, given what you've learned so far. You're already familiar with the idea of an MVP. Now I want to introduce you to the alpha test—AKA field test, longitudinal test, or pilot test.

At this early stage, it's super-useful to sketch out what your alpha test might look like. Once you've validated your ideas and collected customer data, you'll update and iterate your alpha test plan with more details and insights about your product and audience.

Software Release Cycles

In software development, there are four common stages:

- **Pre-alpha:** all the activities that happen before any software testing, including customer discovery, project planning, requirements gathering, task analysis, competitive analysis, etc.

- **Alpha:** an early, incomplete version of your product that includes core systems.

- **Beta:** a feature-complete version that needs testing, tuning and debugging.

- **Release:** software that's been debugged and is ready to release to the public.

Many entrepreneurs are eager to release a product quickly, so they can get feedback on their idea, but if you're building something meaningful and substantial, a private alpha test with a handful of early hot-core customers can get you much further, much faster—and set you up for long-term success.

Sketch Out Your Alpha Test

In the spirit of **_start at the end and work backwards_**, you're going to sketch out your current ideas for running a high-learning alpha test. This will be a multi-week test of your core systems, involving 25–50 people over 4–8 weeks.

Ask yourself:

- What's the earliest version of our product we could use in a 4-week test?

- Who are the 25–50 people who would make great test subjects and have the time and motivation to participate in this test? Where would we find them?

- Which assumptions will we test during alpha? What signals will determine if these assumptions are validated?

The purposes of asking these questions up-front is to get you thinking ahead, and to help you focus and streamline your efforts during the rest of this program. You don't have all the answers right now—and that's OK. Here's a template to get you started.

Alpha research plan

WHO: [XX] people with [YY] characteristics .

WHAT: an [X]-week Alpha test designed to test [Assumptions 1, 2, 3]

WHEN: [XX] days from [gating event]]

WHERE: [geographic location: online, in-person, etc.]

WHY: get early feedback on our core systems and features.

There is no one-size-fits-all alpha test format. For Happify and Pley, we created alpha test plans to suit each project's needs. Happify's goal was to test a working version of the product, so we brought customers into our offices in New York City for testing.

---

happify Alpha research plan

WHO: moms with young kids who recently left the workforce.

WHAT: four-week test of a single activity with the game (early version).

WHEN: once a crude version of that single activity is built and ready.

WHERE: in-person, in our New York City offices.

WHY: test the appeal and fun factor in our core offering. Do they like it?

Pley's Alpha goal was to test an idea for an online video community using YouTube. So we created an online test plan to support that goal.

---

pley Alpha research plan

WHO: subscribers with young kids who love sharing photos online.

WHAT: four-weeks of content and contests in Pley's YouTube channel.

WHEN: once we produce the content and organize the contests.

WHERE: online, via YouTube.

WHY: validate our idea for family-friendly educational content.

Even though you don't yet know how your research will unfold, you'll get tremendous benefit from imagining how an alpha test could work, and who will be in it.

If you plan your research and design activities working backwards from that goal, your design efforts will become more focused and streamlined. Plus, this will set you up for your next task: finding and empathizing with your hot-core superfans.

Worksheet: Product Brief (Draft)

Now it's your turn. Answer these questions to draft your product brief.

Include Your Before MVP Canvas and Elevator Pitch

Begin your product brief with the MVP canvas and elevator pitch that you wrote in the Chapter 1 worksheet.

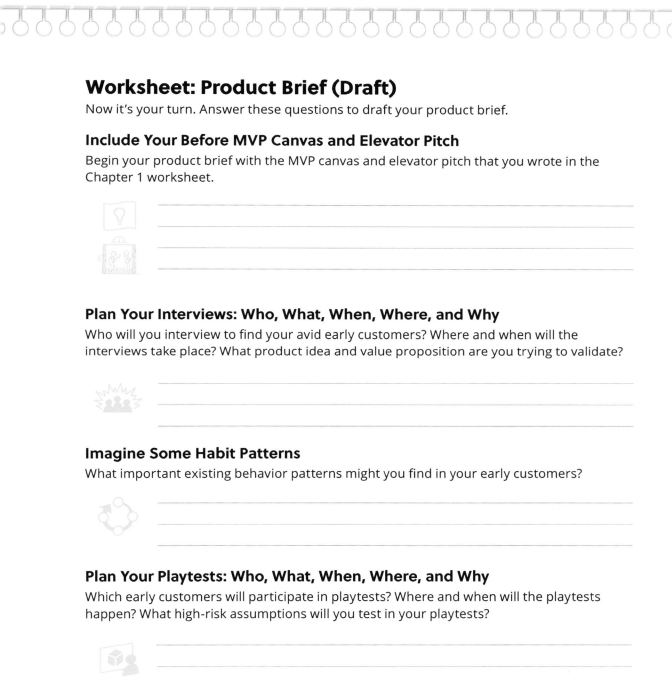

Plan Your Interviews: Who, What, When, Where, and Why

Who will you interview to find your avid early customers? Where and when will the interviews take place? What product idea and value proposition are you trying to validate?

Imagine Some Habit Patterns

What important existing behavior patterns might you find in your early customers?

Plan Your Playtests: Who, What, When, Where, and Why

Which early customers will participate in playtests? Where and when will the playtests happen? What high-risk assumptions will you test in your playtests?

Product Brief Speed Bumps

Speed bump #1: Lack of internal support

If your organization is unfamiliar with hypothesis-driven testing, you'll get pushback. This happens when your colleagues don't have the skill set and experience to run these tests, so they dismiss what they don't understand. Or perhaps they've absorbed the "launch fast and see what happens" ethos of lean startup without understanding the discipline that leads up to a successful launch.

To meet this challenge head-on, **find and educate an internal champion** who can help you get resources and support. Ideally, try to partner with someone who's eager to learn cutting-edge techniques that lead to breakthrough innovations, and who is willing to shepherd your project through completion.

Speed bump #2: Lack of focus on a small early market

The surest way to derail early product development is to go broad and build for everyone—which usually delights nobody. If you can't get your team to focus on a small, specific early market, it will be tough to innovate successfully. This is often the result of a well-meaning mass market visionary who thinks big but doesn't know how to get there.

The superfan funnel gets around this problem by showing you how to find the right customers for product discovery and testing. **Use the superfan funnel to focus on a handful of early testers.** Work with your internal champion to get the support and resources you need to make this happen.

Speed bump #3: Overdeveloping software too early

Although you and your team might have the best intentions, it's emotionally difficult in practice to let potential customers interact with a buggy, ugly version of your grand vision. Many startups set out to build their alpha, but end up developing and polishing something that's much closer to a beta. This subverts your golden opportunity for early feedback and can lock you into a direction that may or may not be optimal.

The best way I've seen to avoid this trap is to **articulate EXACTLY what you want to learn and lay out the quickest, cheapest way to learn that**.

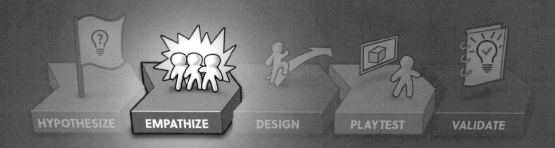

SECTION II
Empathize

Build something just a few people want—even if most people don't get it right away.

Paul Buchheit, Partner in Y Combinator

Trying to please everyone is the surest way to fail. To deliver a compelling product experience, you need to target specific people and understand their needs.

Empathizing with customers is a cornerstone of design thinking and lean UX. In practice, customer empathy can be tricky to pull off. How do you find the right people to empathize with? Who do you listen to and, more importantly, who do you ignore?

Most of us don't have the time or skills to perform ethnographic research with our target customers. Too many times, we end up empathizing with the wrong people and getting insights that lead us astray. But it doesn't have to be that way.

In this section, you'll learn a **proven system for empathizing with your hot-core customers**—the ones who'll help you refine your hypotheses, tune your systems, and increase your odds of success.

Chapter 3

Find Your Hot-Core Superfans

Early adopters will put up with cost, ridicule, and friction to get their needs met.

Erika Hall, Author, *Just Enough Research*

FINDING THE RIGHT EARLY CUSTOMERS is crucial for success, and not easy to do. Most entrepreneurs stumble when they get to this step. They've been told "Get out of the building and go find people to interview" so that's what they do.

But when you cast a broad net, you get muddled feedback. All those glowing comments you hear from your friends, family, and investors—the people who support you and care about you—can be terribly misleading.

Why Focus on Your Early Market?

It takes focus, energy, and humility to proactively connect with a small, nascent market of early customers. Why bother? Because the payoff is huge. Your early adopters can:

- playtest your early versions without needing a lot of hand-holding.
- give you articulate feedback on early versions of your systems and features.
- help you bring your core social systems to life during alpha and beyond.
- evangelize your beta program and spread the word when you're ready to scale.

How to Find Your Superfans

When you set out to create something new, you need to seek out feedback from a **specific type of customer with four key characteristics:**

Superfan characteristics

They **HAVE** the problem that you want to solve.

They **KNOW** they have the problem—it's top-of-mind.

They're trying to **SOLVE** the problem by seeking out current options.

They're **DISSATISFIED** with those options and want something better.

I call these people **superfans**. That's shorthand for **high-need, high-value early customers. High-need** because they have a burning need or desire for what you're creating, perhaps for reasons you don't yet understand. **High-value** because they're articulate, observant, and have the motivation and energy to help you bring your product to life. In other words, they would be excellent alpha testers.

The Many Benefits of Superfans

Research from the Nielsen/Norman group suggests that you only need five testers to know if you're on the right track. But here's the catch: they need to be the *right* five people for your product and development stage.

In the early stages of product development, you'll get more value from five superfans than dozens of so-called "target customers" who fit your profile and think your product is cool. **Once you delight your superfans, you're onto something that can grow.** But if you're missing this early, energetic human feedback loop, it's almost impossible to "cross the chasm" into mainstream use.

Working on *Rock Band*, for example, we knew that to bring the game to life, we'd have to first capture the hearts and minds of hardcore music gamers—early, passionate customers with a burning desire for more and better music games. So long before beta, we had eager testers provide input and create content that would make the game more fun for everyone.

Superfans are pre-chasm early adopters.
They don't need social proof before trying something new, because their need or desire is so great. This is who you're looking for: people who actively feel the pain of *not* having what you offer.

Write Your Superfan Screener

Now you're going to learn a technique for sifting the wheat from the chaff called a **superfan screener**, This short, six-question survey is designed to attract people who *could be* your early customers. This is stage 1 of your superfan funnel. When combined with Stages 2 and 3, the screener gives you a powerful system for validating and testing early ideas with exactly the right customers.

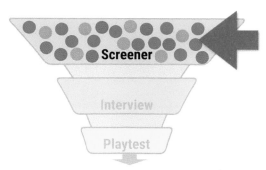

Choose Your Recruiting Channels

There are many channels available for recruiting subjects. Which one is the best way to reach your early adopters? That depends on your current relationship with your potential customers.

A good rule of thumb is to **go where potential superfans hang out** to recruit them. Here are some channels to consider, along with guidelines for when to use them. Try to pursue several channels in parallel, in case one doesn't work out or moves slowly.

Direct email. If you have a list of existing customers or fans, you can email them directly and invite them to take your screener. If you have a large list and usage data, try reaching out to the most relevant active subset of your list first. Ranan Lachman at Pley used this technique to recruit customers who were actively sharing photos online—a proxy for people who might want to be part of an online community.

Friend-of-friend social media sharing. Social media sharing is another great way to find research subjects. You can share your outreach message yourself—but it's even more effective to use the friend-of-friend (FOF) technique, and ask your friends and colleagues to share your message. This will help you reach outside of your network, and find subjects who don't know you personally and are less likely to want to please you (and will thus be more honest).

Recruiting ads on Craigslist, Facebook, or Google. If you're targeting a vertical such as passionate hobbyists, harried students, or overworked parents, you can often get high-quality survey leads by placing ads on sites like Craigslist, Facebook, or Google. Keep in mind that you'll need to filter out "professional research subjects," who will say whatever they think will secure the gig (that's what speed interviews are for).

Interest groups. Do you belong to interest groups on LinkedIn, Facebook, or other online communities? Those groups can be a great place to find superfans. Be sure to provide value to the group before posting your recruiting message, and check with the group leader to make sure your message will be welcome. If you don't belong to these groups already, you can join one and establish yourself—or ask a friend who belongs to relevant groups to post a message on your behalf.

Meetups and conferences. Although recruiting subject online is convenient and scalable, you can also get great results from recruiting face-to-face. If there are meetups in your area, you can give a presentation that includes an offer to participate in your study at the end.

If you're visiting a conference with a large concentration of potential superfans, you can take advantage of that by recruiting people into your survey before and during the conference. You can ask them to take an online survey, or simply ask your questions in person and note their response. SAAS entrepreneur Megan Mahdavi used this approach to screen potential superfans at Dreamforce, a huge yearly Salesforce event.

Paid research services. If you're short on time or don't have the resources to recruit subjects yourself, you can reach out to paid research services with a detailed description of who you're looking for, and they can deliver subjects who fit that description. Although this can be expensive, it's sometimes the best way to find exactly the types of people you're looking for.

Write Your Recruiting Message

Before you send out your survey, you'll write a short message that describes who you're looking for and what you're offering. Here's a template to get your started.

Recruiting message

Hello! We are looking for [men and women] age [XX-YY] who are [key characteristics of your Superfans] to participate in [paid] research studies for a new [high-level product description].

If you're selected for the study, you will earn [$XX/hour] as thanks for your time. To apply for the study, take this quick screener:

    <link to screener>

Thanks! We look forward to hearing from you soon.

Sincerely, [name and title]

Here are two sample outreach messages aimed at different recruiting channels.

Happify message posted on parenting websites in NYC, SF & LA:
We're looking for tech-savvy parents 25–45 who own a smartphone, have purchased self-help books or programs in the past, and are eager to learn and practice daily habits that are scientifically proven to boost your happiness.

Pley email sent to existing subscribers:
We're looking for Lego-loving parents who enjoy sharing pictures and messages, and want to help us improve our service by developing a more vibrant community.

Laura Klein on Picking the Right People

Laura Klein is a customer development ninja. She runs the *Users Know* website and is the author of *Build Better Products* and *UX for Lean Startups*.

Pick the right people to talk to. If you're building a product for astronauts, don't waste your time talking to people who aren't astronauts. You're not going to get any good feedback. In fact, you might get feedback that sends you in exactly the wrong direction.

Don't build a product "for moms." There are too many of them. They are too dissimilar from each other and it's impossible to build something that every single one of them will like.

Pick a very specific group of people that you can actually talk to and start seeing patterns. That will save you so much time.

Write Your Screener Questions

Now, write a short screening survey designed to identify early customers. Try starting with six questions—three multiple choice, three open-ended—then tweak the survey to fit your project's needs. Here are some tips for writing an effective superfan screener.

- **The shorter your survey, the more responses you'll get.** Resist the urge to ask everything—focus instead on asking only the questions that sort your responses and identify your superfans.

- **Behavior is a stronger signal than belief.** For multiple-choice questions, think about which behaviors could identify them as superfans—and ask questions about those behaviors.

- **Superfans are actively trying to solve their problem.** To identify high-need customers, include open-ended questions that reveal what that person is doing to solve their problem, scratch their itch, or meet their need. As a bonus, you may get some competitive analysis of your space.

- **Superfans have opinions about how things could be better.** Include at least one question that invites self-reflection, such as asking how things could be improved.

Here is a sample survey, from our customer insights research with Pley.

Pley superfan screener

MULTIPLE CHOICE

What is your age range?

How many kids are living with you? What ages?

How often per week does your family play with Legos?

OPEN-ENDED

Which online social communities do you participate in?

Do you seek out Lego-related websites or apps specifically?

How could these websites and apps be more effective for you?

We chose demographic questions that would surface the respondents' family situation and play patterns, two important factors that differentiated existing subscribers.

We wanted to talk with both men and women, so we left the gender question out of the survey. We also wanted to find people who were comfortable with using digital communities—a good proxy for our early adopter—so we included open-ended questions about their current use, and requested their ideas about improving the websites and communities they already participate in.

Multiple-Choice Questions Surface Patterns

It takes focus to listen to your early market. You need to say no to some opportunities, and yes to others. If your customer hypothesis contains specific targeting questions, this survey is a great time to start gathering insight and feedback.

Pley knew that their adult subscribers without kids had very different needs from families with kids. So Pley included survey questions about the number and age of kids in each household to gauge interest and need for a digital community for both families and kid-free adults.

Open-Ended Questions Reveal Motivation

It's likely that you'll filter out some respondents using their multiple-choice answers. Maybe they're too young, too old, too unfamiliar with the product space, don't have the right smartphone, or don't use a specific tool often enough.

For people who make it through your demographic filter, their open-ended answers contain clues you'll need to identify enthusiastic early adopters, and spot the respondents who don't fit your needs. Make your open-ended questions relevant and revealing.

Run Your Survey With a Time Limit

Next, choose a survey platform and collect some data. Two great options are Google Forms and Survey Monkey, but any platform you're comfortable with will do.

In practice, most survey responses come in within 24 hours of posting. To get the best response, give your respondents a deadline—say, 24 or 48 hours from the date you send or post it—and tell them to fill out the survey immediately. Be sure to post your survey during a time when your respondents are usually available.

Filter Subjects and Identify Patterns

Once you've collected around 50–100 survey responses, you'll need to filter these responses and decide which ones will pass through the funnel. I recommend the stoplight method to filter survey responses in three buckets. Here's how it works.

Red = No. They fell outside of your focus (age, gender, location) and/or they submitted minimal open-ended answers.

Yellow = Maybe. They work as a backup. Perhaps they gave short or minimal answers, or got mixed reviews from team members.

Green = Yes. They gave relevant, thought-provoking responses, and you're eager to hear more from them.

Most people like to color-code the rows in their survey response spreadsheet using green, yellow, and red. If you're in a hurry, you can focus initially on green-lighting the best dozen or so respondents for quick follow-up, then process the rest later.

Document Three to Five Key Response Patterns

Once you've color-coded your responses, sit down with your team and look for emergent patterns in the data. Look for beliefs, habits, desires, or pain points related to your area of interest that show up in several responses, not just one or two.

When analyzing data, it can be tough to see what's actually there, especially when it's unexpected.

In our Pley interviews. for example, we learned that many of our subscribers were frustrated with Pley's set reviews, and wanted help in choosing the right toy for their child—something that surprised us, but we paid attention—and documenting this finding helped the Pley team prioritize some improvements to set reviews, and bump it to the top of their development queue.

Green-Light 10–15 Early Adopters

Once you've filtered your results, it's time to make a green-light list of 10–15 respondents who have the qualities you're looking for. For example, Pley's green-light list contained about a dozen Lego-addicted dads and moms with these characteristics:

- active builders, renting multiple sets per month.

- kids are Lego-obsessed—it's their favorite activity.

- like to build during the day and watch Lego-building videos at night.

Happify's green-light list contained around 20 women with these characteristics:

- stay-at-home Moms who'd recently left the workforce.

- caring for young or school-aged children.

- motivated to improve their mood and become happier and more upbeat.

Your green-light list will contain a filtered list of people who could be hot-core early adopters. In the next chapter, you'll learn how to filter that list while gathering high-value insights that inform your product design.

Worksheet: Superfan Screener

Now it's your turn. Answer these questions to plan your search for early customers.

Early Customer Hypotheses

Who has a burning need for your product, and can also give you useful feedback on early prototypes? If you have several hypotheses, write them all down.

_____

_____

_____

_____

Competitive Analysis

Who else is trying to fill this need, and why are they falling short?

_____

_____

_____

_____

Recruiting Channels

Which groups, venues, channels, or events might be good places for you to recruit possible early customers?

_____

_____

_____

_____

_____

_____

Recruiting Message

Write an outreach message to recruit people who would be interested in participating in a paid playtest for a new product.

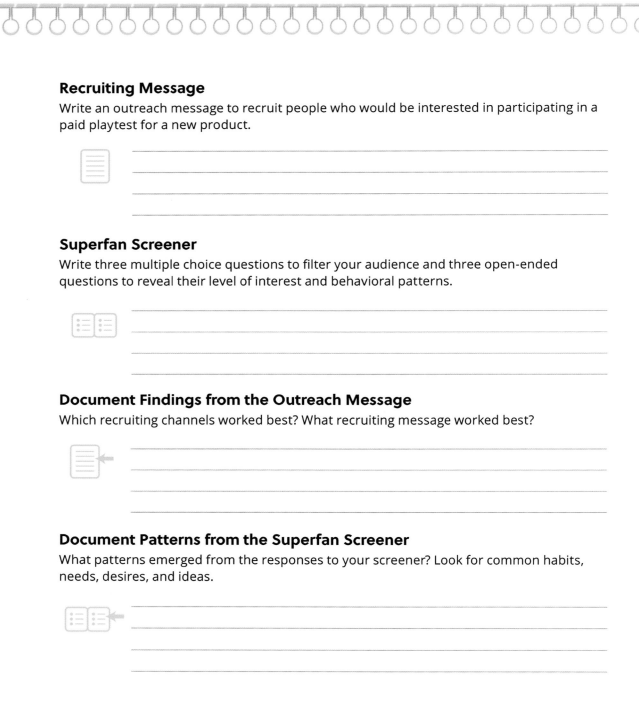

Superfan Screener

Write three multiple choice questions to filter your audience and three open-ended questions to reveal their level of interest and behavioral patterns.

Document Findings from the Outreach Message

Which recruiting channels worked best? What recruiting message worked best?

Document Patterns from the Superfan Screener

What patterns emerged from the responses to your screener? Look for common habits, needs, desires, and ideas.

Rank Respondents

Categorize respondents into three groups: green=definitely interview them, yellow=maybe, red=no.

Follow-up Message

Write a message inviting green-light respondents to schedule 5-minute interviews.

Write a message politely declining yellow- and red-light respondents.

Superfan Speed Bumps

As you're identifying your hot-core superfans, watch out for these speed bumps and don't let 'em slow you down.

Speed bump #1: Mismatched recruiting channel

Again, a common stumbling block in customer research is finding the right recruiting channel to pull in early adopters.

To keep channel-mismatch problems from slowing you down, **calibrate promising channels with a few small recruiting experiments**—and then double down on what works.

Speed bump #2: Ineffective recruiting message

If you're getting a poor response to your message, or if you get too many non-targeted responses outside of your target, rewrite your recruiting message and try it again. (The templates we provide are merely a starting point.)

To avoid this, you can **A/B test your recruiting message** to find what works. Try writing two or three different recruiting messages and measure which ones get better, more targeted responses.

Speed bump #3: The pile-on

If you work in a larger company or a tight-knit startup culture, you may experience "the pile-on." That's when colleagues outside of your project find out that you're running a survey and just want to "slip one or two questions in." Doing this will change your response rate and muddy up your data.

Don't allow random questions into your survey. Instead say, "There will be other surveys. This one is short and focused on finding specific people."

Chapter 4

Surface Relevant Habits and Needs

Learning without research is just guessing.
Laura Klein, Author, *Build Better Products*

PRIOR TO BUILDING ANYTHING, THE BEST WAY to get feedback on your value proposition is to interview potential customers and learn about their habits and needs. These "discovery interviews" can take different forms:

Where: meet in person, chat by phone, or video-chat on Skype or Google Hangouts.

When: talk for five minutes, twenty minutes, or an hour.

What: ask scripted questions or have a free-form discussion.

Any of these techniques can be useful, **as long as you're interviewing the right people.** That's the hard part. Who do you focus on, and who do you ignore?

Innovation diffusion theory gives us a road map for which customers to focus on first: our pre-chasm early market. When you're bringing a new idea to life, pay attention to feedback from your early market and ignore the rest.

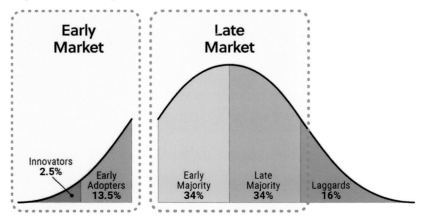

Easier said than done. It's tricky to differentiate between the market segments on either side of the chasm. In practice, early adopters can look an awful lot like early majority. How do we tell which is which? Here's a handy differentiator:

Early adopters don't need social proof or convincing to try something.
They're delighted to discover your offering and help you shape it, because it solves a real problem or fulfills a desire that they KNOW they have.

Early majority are pragmatists who look for social proof before jumping in.
They consider themselves forward-thinking and will try something if others they admire try it first. If their pain point becomes great enough, they may cross the chasm **backwards** and become early adopters.

Surface Customer Insights with Speed Interviews

In the previous chapter, you learned how to create a screener that will attract the right hot-core early customers for your product, service, or business.

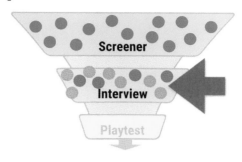

Now you're going to learn a powerful technique—Stage 2 in your superfan funnel—called speed interviews. These short conversations will identify excellent playtest subjects, and surface customer insights that will accelerate your product design process.

Short, Revealing Conversations

Speed interviews are 5- to 10-minute conversations that are designed to:

1. identify articulate, enthusiastic testers for your product.

2. surface relevant patterns and insights about your early market—habits, beliefs, pain points, and unmet needs that can influence your early product thinking.

To run speed interviews, you need a filtered list of potential superfans,

Reach Out to Your Green-Light Screener Candidates

Now you're going to contact people and let them know that you'd like to ask a few follow-up screening questions. The best place to start is your green-light screener list—the people who gave the most relevant answers to your open-ended questions.

If you already have a list of customers or fans to work with, incorporate that right into this process.

If you advertised online for paid research, this step is how you screen out "professional research subjects" who are looking for paid research opportunities and saying what they think you want to hear. These folks will often fail to respond to a follow-up screening interview, because it's is too much trouble. And if they do come to the interview, you can spot them quickly and screen them out.

True early adopters will be eager to share their opinions and talk about something they care about. They might appreciate the money, but their real motivation is a chance to share their opinion and be heard.

Here's an email template to use as a starting point for reaching out to your list.

Screener follow-up letter

Dear [recipient],

Thanks for taking our survey. We got a tremendous response—more than we expected—and your answers were among the best. Now we need to select 10 people for our first few rounds of testing. We're conducting 5–10-minute screen interviews via phone or Skype, and we're excited to speak with you and see if you're a good fit.

This will be quick and convenient. Please book a time in the calendar that works for you: <link to scheduling tool>

Thanks! We look forward to speaking with you soon.

Sincerely, [name and title]

Be sure to customize this to make sense for your context and customers.

5–10 Minutes, 2–3 Questions

In a speed interview, you ask a few revealing questions that follow up on the themes you introduced in the screener. How do you decide which questions to ask? A great place to start is with the response patterns that bubbled up in your screener—the habits, ideas, beliefs, and unmet needs that surprised you, intrigued you, and made you want to know more. Those early clues can lead you down a path that may either support or challenge your product assumptions and cherished beliefs. Either way, it's good info to have as you're exploring your early market and shaping your ideas.

Setup Half-Hour Time Slots for Your Interviews

Even though you'll be speaking to them for 5–10 minutes, book half-hour slots for the interviews. That will give you the flexibility you need for late starts, tech troubleshooting, and post-interview debriefing with your team. Trust me: You'll be glad you did.

Keep It Short and Professional

Unlike exploratory interviews, speed interviews are highly focused and designed to calibrate whether that person could be a useful tester. If your questions are strong, you'll know within a few minutes if you want to talk with this person further. Keep it short and professional; you'll get better, more actionable data. You should leave the interview wanting to hear more from your best subjects.

Erika Hall on The Art of Listening

Erika Hall is the co-founder of Mule Design and the author of *Conversational Design* and *Just Enough Research*.

The most important thing to remember when you are interviewing potential customers is to be quiet. A lot of people think interviewing is asking good questions and demonstrating your skill as an interviewer. But if you find the right person, your job is get out of the way and let that person talk.

Don't worry too much about asking exactly the right questions. Let silence happen. Remember that you want to learn about things you might not have even thought to ask.

Don't make the mistake I did—running long when the interview is going well. I had a great conversation once with a subject who was particularly forthcoming until he mentioned that we'd planned for 10 minutes and had taken 25. After that, he no longer trusted me to stick to time limits in the future. Oops. I won't make that mistake again.

Tweak Your Questions to Maximize Learning

Speed interviews are a great place to practice lightweight, iterative learning. During your first few interviews, you'll quickly learn which questions are most revealing and which ones are duds. Don't be afraid to tweak your interview script to focus on the best questions and to throw out or change the others. That's the beauty of this technique: You're looking for emergent patterns and customer insights, and you have freedom and flexibility in how you gather that data.

Screening Questions for Finding Superfans

Screening interviews are a great way to get quick, actionable data that can help you test your assumptions and design the right MVP. Here are four screening questions that will surface your superfans and reveal actionable customer insights.

Walk us through your typical day. How does [relevant activity] fit into your day?

This question will help you assess whether there's a top-of-mind pain point in their lives you can meet. Many times, people will volunteer details you want to know. When they do, sit back and listen. It's okay to guide them with follow-up questions, but only when there's something specific you need to know. For example, if you're planning to prototype using a specific platform, you can ask about which devices, apps, and websites they use to pursue that activity, and this information can help you decide where to reach your early market.

What solutions have you tried to solve this problem? How'd that work for you?

We know that actions speak louder than words, and this question will separate true early adopters from the pack. This is where you find out what actions they're already taking to solve their problem or quench their desire. For a diabetes solution, you'd ask about which current solutions for managing diabetes they've tried and how those solutions affected (or didn't affect) their lives.

Are your solutions working? How would life be different if this worked better?

This question will help you assess the strength and urgency of their unmet need or desire. Is there a real pain point in their lives that you can meet? You'll tune it to work for your situation. In the case of a diabetes solution, you'd dig into their frustration with current solutions, and how that's impacting their life.

How could [relevant activity] be better or easier? What's missing?

This question is a great way to end your interview. What's their appetite for improvement? Do they volunteer new ideas? Ask what they'd improve, what's missing, what could be better.

Not everybody thinks this way. Some people just accept things as they are, and don't volunteer ideas for improvement. You want to find the ones that do have ideas and want to be part of making things better.

Run Interviews with a Partner

Run these interviews solo if you must, but you'll get better results if you run them with a partner or team. During the first interview, have one person ask questions while another takes notes and identifies emergent patterns. Then switch it up. Have someone else take notes, and a new person run the interview. This will give you multiple pairs of eyes on the emergent patterns, which generates better results. Plus, you'll train your team to feel comfortable using these time-saving skills.

Interviewer   Subject

Notetaker

Analyze Your data and Choose Your Testers

Once you've completed the interviews, get together with your team and look across the data for relevant emergent patterns. Once you have combed through the data, you'll have a sense for who'd make good testers. Choose articulate people who gave thoughtful answers—and who represent an important segment of your early market.

Use the red/yellow/green method from Chapter 2 to quickly mark up your data. To identify greens, ask yourself: Am I eager to hear more from this person? Do I want to know what she thinks about our product? If you can't wait to hear more, you've found a good tester.

Speed Interviews for Pley

Pley's green-light list was filled with parents who had an urgent need to "feed the habit" of their Lego-loving kids.

In our interviews, we followed up on patterns we'd surfaced during the screening survey. We put together a set of questions and interviewed families via Skype with their kids so we could see how the family interacts with the computer.

Here are the questions we asked.

- Walk us through a typical day-in-the-life of your household. How do Lego-related activities fit into your day? How do you feed your kids' Lego habit?

- Do your kids use Lego-related sites or apps? How often? When?

- What are the high and low points of your Lego-related experiences?

- How could these experiences be better/easier/happier? What's missing? If you had a magic wand, what would you change?

What we learned from the data was *not* what we were hoping to hear: Parents lack the time and interest for yet another hobbyist community. This refuted Pley's solution hypotheses, so we dug deeper to see what they *did* want. We learned that parents use videos as a benevolent babysitter, but worry about exposing their kids to adult content. These early-adopter parents asked for creative instructional videos to help their kids get more fun out of each rental set.

Bingo! That unmet customer need is connected to Pley's key success metric: increasing the rental period. We paid attention, and those customer insights became the centerpiece of a successful MVP strategy for the Pley community.

Worksheet: Speed Interviews

Now it's your turn. Prepare questions to ask green-light respondents.

Day in the Life

"Walk us through your typical experience of [relevant activity]. How does [relevant activity] fit into your day?"

What's Working Now

"As you do [relevant activity], what [websites, apps, games, services] do you use? Which parts of that experience are working for you? What do you enjoy about that?"

Better than Before

"How could your experience with [relevant activity] be better, easier, or more fulfilling? What's missing, or confusing, or frustrating? If you could wave a magic wand, what would you change?"

Follow-Up Questions

Ask questions to follow up on remarks in screener responses, to help you decide whether to green-light respondents.

Interviewing Speed Bumps

Watch out for these speed bumps while you're running and analyzing your speed interviews.

Speed bump #1: Interview runs long

It's tempting to keep asking questions when your subject is forthcoming, but then you run of risk of exceeding your interview time. To keep your interviews short and professional, **focus on just a few revealing questions**. You should leave the conversation eager to hear more.

Remember, these are screening interviews—you'll have ample time to go deeper with your testers later on.

Speed bump #2: Leading questions skew the results.

These discovery interviews are about understanding habits, needs, and pain points. Don't pitch your solution or ask about pricing models. It'll detour the conversation and skew your results.

Your job is to **become an expert at pattern-matching**. When you're combing through the results, look for the patterns that are actually there, not just the ones you're hoping to see.

Speed bump #3: Interviewer gets personal

It takes supreme self-control to respond unemotionally when someone trashes—or gushes over—your core beliefs. But an emotional reaction will dramatically skew your data and throw off your experiment. If this happens, first forgive yourself for being human, then try being a notetaker and pattern-spotter and let another team member drive the interviews.

When you're interviewing customers, **think like a scientist, not a salesperson**. Be a polite, dispassionate, and objective interviewer. Don't let your emotions drive the conversation; give your subjects space for their emotions to come out and dominate the conversation. That's the way to get honest, actionable data.

Chapter 5

Distill Customer Insights into Job Stories

Job stories make you focus on motivation and context.
Alan Klement, Author, *When Coffee and Kale Compete*

CONGRATULATIONS! YOU JUST LEARNED HOW to find your superfans and discover what these early hot-core customers want and need. Now it's time to **apply those insights to your product.**

To do that, you need to synthesize what you learned into a form that you can use to drive design decisions.

User Stories ≠ Job Stories

At this juncture, many people stumble a bit. Often, they'll turn their insights into "user stories," that are directly tied to product features.

If you've worked in an Agile environment, you know that user stories often end up being an expression of what the engineer wants to build. That leaves a gap between what gets built and what comes out of a person's mouth during your superfan interviews. Remember: **you're not building features yet.** You're working to **understand *core customer needs, habits, and frustrations.***

Job Stories Turn Insights into Action

There's a better way to map your key insights into a design-ready form that your product team can use. They're called *job stories*.

I first learned about job stories from Paul Adams at Intercom. Paul and his team developed this concept based on the "Jobs to Be Done" (JTBD) movement started by Clayton Christensen and others. A job story is a special kind of customer story—told from the customer's POV—that follows the format shown here.

Job story

WHEN [trigger] — something happens: external, internal, situational

I WANT TO [action] — a small act within a larger purpose

SO I CAN [desired outcome] — the value propositon or payoff

Unlike personas, job stories are action-oriented. They capture context and motivation, and will help you distill your research insights and build your product better and faster.

Surface Patterns in the Data

To transform your customer data into actionable insights, start by scanning the data for patterns that are relevant to your product. In particular, look for:

- Existing habits

- Unmet needs

- Pain points

- Ideas or suggestions

Watch Out for Researcher Bias

Researcher bias (AKA looking for a specific outcome) is difficult to manage. If you're passionate about your product idea, your emotions can easily take over and muddy the waters. This can skew your analysis and hamper your search for the truth.

To counteract this natural tendency, **notice patterns in the data**, not just the things you're looking for and would love to confirm. Even better, get several people with differing degrees of emotional investment to look at the data too. If you all see the same patterns, that's a sign that you're successfully combatting researcher bias.

Capture Key Insights with Job Stories

Once you've surfaced key patterns from your research, create job stories that capture those insights in actionable form.

For example, during our Happify research, we learned that frazzled moms like to browse through beautiful, escapist images on Pinterest after drop-off.

WHEN I get the kids off to daycare and have a moment to myself
I WANT TO look through beautiful images of a home life I aspire to
SO I CAN feel inspired, and escape the drudgery of my daily routine.

Paul Adams on Job Stories

Paul Adams is a Dublin-based designer, researcher and VP Product at the customer communications company Intercom.

The job stories thing happened by accident. We were looking at Clay Christensen's jobs-to-be-done theory, and tried applying it to our work. We came up with a formula to describe how something should work: "when I want to <motivation>, I want to <action>, so I can <expected outcome>". For example, "when I sign up for a service, I want to introduce myself so I can ensure that they feel like we care."

I wrote a blog post on visual design, with an addendum on job stories. People jumped on job stories as a pragmatic, practical tool, and they took off.

We still use job stories today. We'll use them at the high level at an early stage in a project. Then we use them as a check in along the way.

Job stories keep us honest.

During our Pley research, we discovered that parents with Lego-obsessed kids were desperate for a guilt-free break and frustrated with the wide-open nature of YouTube.

> **WHEN I** want to grab a few minutes to relax after my workday
>
> **I WANT TO** let my Lego-obsessed kid watch videos unsupervised
>
> **SO I CAN** relax guilt-free without worrying about inappropriate.

During our *Covet Fashion* research, we noticed that fashion-savvy women love to collaborate with one special BFF or family member when getting dressed for an important event.

> **WHEN I** need to dress for an important event
>
> **I WANT TO** raid my friend's closet and get her advice on my outfit
>
> **SO I CAN** have her accessorize my look and help me feel confident.

Pay Attention to Emotions

All these job stories have something in common: an emotional arc that moves the protagonist from one state to another. There's an implicit emotion embedded in the trigger, and **the desired outcome has an emotional component** that tells you the state they're seeking to change.

Happify Mom moves from FRAZZLED to CALM

by immersing herself in beautiful, escapist, inspiring visuals

Pley Dad moves from GUILTY to RELAXED by giving

his kid unsupervised access to educational Lego videos.

The Covet Fashionista moves from ANXIOUS to CONFIDENT by playing dress-up with a close friend or family member, so she can feel supported and confident in her fashion choices.

Emotional Arcs Drive Your Customer's Experience

These emotional arcs drive your customer's experience, and provide the underpinnings of a delightful customer experience.

Engaging your superfans with emotions

- **Start by** understanding your superfans' habits and frustrations.
- **Write job stories** that capture these emotions and unmet needs.
- **Design your product** to bring these arcs to satisfying conclusions.

Piggyback on Existing Habits

Don't fall into the common trap of thinking that your innovative offering will create brand-new habits. If you want to drive adoption and retention, it's easier to piggyback on an existing habit than get someone to build an entirely new one, just for your product.

This is the reason you floss when you brush your teeth: It's easier to remember, and the actions group together into a single habit.

During your research, **pay special attention when your subjects talk about existing habits that are relevant to your offering.** Daily habits are important, but so are weekly, monthly, and even seasonal or yearly ones. All can be potential hooks for driving long-term engagement.

Habit stories are a special type of job story built around an existing habit and an unmet need. This powerful tool will help you identify promising opportunities for delivering customer value and driving reengagement.

Every story contains triggers—the cues and reminders that drive customers into habitual behaviors. As we explored earlier, your job stories have an emotional arc that begins with a trigger.

Jesse Schell on Listening to Customers

Jesse Schell is a game designer and CEO of Schell Games, an education/entertainment game design company. He is a professor of Entertainment Technology at Carnegie Mellon University.

I remember when we created Pixie Hollow, a massively multi-player game for girls based on Tinkerbell. We had a whole design worked out that we felt pretty good about. We said, "Before we get into any production, let's talk to girls and see how they feel about it."

We didn't tell the girls, "Here's what we're thinking." We asked really simple questions, like, "If you were a fairy, what would you do?" We thought we knew the answer. We were wrong. The answer was, "Fly."

We hadn't been thinking about flying because we'd been focused on the Tinkerbell movie, where flying isn't prominently featured. We immediately changed our plan. We made it so you're flying every second of the game.

Early conversations can be really important.

Habit Stories Start with Situational Triggers

Now think about **situational triggers**—the transitions, rituals, and events that structure your customer's daily life and appear in your job stories. For example:

The Happify mom gets home after morning drop-off and faces dirty dishes.

The Pley parent gets home from work and wants to have a drink with his wife.

The *Covet* fashionista has a blind date coming up and wants her friend's input.

Think back and identify the most relevant situational triggers in your data. That will help you surface habit stories that will help you design a compelling mastery path and learning loop (Section III).

Pair Your Job Stories with Customer Quotes

As you've synthesizing your key insights, you need a clear, concise way to communicate what you're learning to your team and stakeholders. Story–quote pairs are a great way to synthesize what you learned. To create one, select a job story that captures a key finding, and illustrate it with a quote (or paraphrase) from a subject.

The Happify mom gets home in the morning after drop-off and faces dirty dishes.

WHEN I get the kids off to daycare and have a moment to myself
I WANT TO look through beautiful images of a home life I aspire to
SO I CAN feel inspired, and escape the drudgery of my daily routine.

I love to browse Pinterest when I'm feeling blue, and get inspired.

The Pley parent gets home from work and wants to have a drink with his wife.

WHEN I want to grab a few minutes to relax after my workday
I WANT TO let my Lego-obsessed kid watch videos unsupervised
SO I CAN relax guilt-free without worrying about inappropriate.

I wish there was a family-friendly YouTube channel for Lego lovers.

The *Covet* **fashionista** has a blind date coming up and wants her friend's input.

WHEN I need to dress for an important event
I WANT TO raid my friend's closet and get her advice on my outfit
SO I CAN have her accessorize my look and help me feel confident.

Nancy is amazing! Her belt is perfect with my outfit.

Job Stories Are a Bridge from Problem Space to Solution Space

I want you to notice something about these job stories: They **express the problem and desired outcome without specifying the solution.**

That's what you're striving for.

Job stories give you a bridge from problem space to solution space. To build that bridge, **make sure your research-based job stories are expressed in problem space**, AKA your customer's existing world—NOT in the solution space you want to draw them into.

We'll use that bridge to move forward into solution space (Section III), where you'll learn to design a compelling product experience using a mastery path, learning loop and social action matrix.

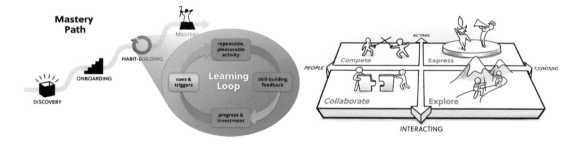

Worksheet: Job Stories

Now it's your turn. Summarize customer insights you gained from the interviews, to prepare your team to design, build, and test your MVP.

Existing Habits

Which habits do early customers already have that are relevant to your product offering?

_____
_____
_____
_____

What unmet needs or pain points are associated with those habits? What itch can your offering scratch?

_____
_____
_____
_____

Job Stories

Capture your customers' needs, emotions, and motivations by writing job stories in this form: "When [trigger], I want to [purposeful activity], so I can [desired outcome]."

_____
_____
_____
_____
_____
_____

Existing Triggers

Note internal and situational triggers that are already in your early customers' lives. What emotions or urges could drive customers to seek out your product?

_____

What transition, chore, event, or ritual could drive customers to return to your product?

_____

Customer Quotations

Illustrate your most promising research-based findings with a customer quote—something that someone actually said or a composite that captures the pattern you're seeing in the data. Pair each quotation with a corresponding job or habit story.

_____

Job Story Speed Bumps

As you distill customer insights, watch out for these speed bumps along the way.

Speed bump #1: Over-reliance on personas

Personas are staples of the design world and can be useful. However, personas can slow you down during early product development, especially when you're trying to focus on your MVP.

Try replacing or supplementing your personas with job stories that **focus your team on motivation and context**—not demographics and implementation.

Speed bump #2: Researcher bias

It takes supreme self-control to absorb feedback that contradicts your own biases, even when you're trying to get the most trustworthy and actionable data you can. You don't need advanced pattern-matching superpowers. You just need to see what's really there.

Be objective, open-minded, and honest about what the data is telling you. If you find that challenging, get someone else to analyze the data and compare notes with you, especially someone who's impartial about the outcome.

Speed bump #3: No existing habits to hook into

If your early research revealed no compelling habit stories, you can still harvest job stories about customer needs. It'll be tough, however, to build something people use regularly, unless you can find an existing, ongoing habit to piggyback on.

If your product doesn't rely on habitual engagement—well, you're off the hook. If it does, you have a choice: **try to build a new habit with your product (difficult but do-able)** OR find a different group of early customers who DO have a habit you can hook onto.

SECTION III
Design

Design is not just what it looks like and feels like. Design is how it works.

Steve Jobs

Now that you've explored problem space and synthesized your customer insights, it's time to move to solution space and design your product experience.

In this section, you'll learn how to map out a compelling experience over time. You'll learn a powerful framework for mapping out a mastery path that improves as your customer becomes more skilled. You'll learn to increase uptake and build engagement by piggybacking on your customers' existing habits. And you'll discover why the best MVP is often a Day 21 Learning Loop.

This framework will help you build your MVP like a game designer would, and "find the fun" in your core product experience. In the next section on playtesting, you'll take these design decisions and decide how to bring your vision to life and test your assumptions.

Chapter 6

Sketch Your Mastery Path

Upgrade your user, not your product—make people better at something they want to get better at.
                    Kathy Sierra, Creator, the Head First series

NOW THAT YOU'VE SYNTHESIZED CUSTOMER INSIGHTS into job stories, it's time to dive into product design. In this chapter, you'll learn how to harness our innate human drive towards progress and mastery, and turn that into product design.

The mastery path tool is based on the four stages of a long-lasting customer experience. Using this tool, you'll sketch out a product experience that helps your customers get better at something they care about—over 30 days, 60 days, and so on.

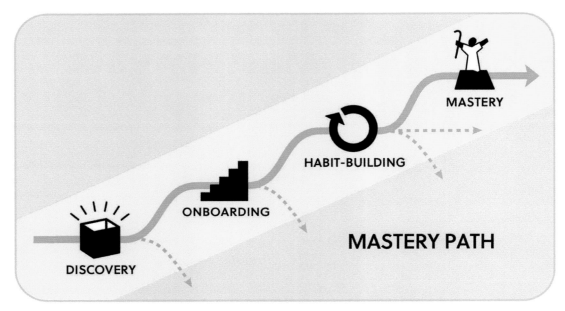

DISCOVERY	ONBOARDING	HABIT-BUILDING	MASTERY
Visitors discover your product, form an impression and decide if they'll check it out.	**Newcomers** take their first steps, learn the ropes, and start getting value from the experience.	**Regulars** re-engage in a cyclic loop that delivers the "hit" they're looking for.	**Experts,** who've built their skills and mastered the system, are ready for something more.

From Customer to Hero

We know from self-determination theory that **people are motivated by meaningful progress.** As you play a game, you gain skills and knowledge that prepare you to take on greater challenges. In storytelling terms, this is a classic **hero's journey.**

In product design terms, you're taking your customers on a **learning journey** that will transform them in some way. **Your customer is the hero of their own story**—the story unfolding inside their head about who they'll become by using your product. What's the story about? How does it unfold?

That's the question your mastery path answers.

A Coherent and Satisfying Whole

In a well-designed game, each stage of the experience is connected to the others, and together the individual elements coalesce into a coherent and satisfying whole. You can see this progression unfold in *Journey*, an emotionally compelling console game.

In the early levels, you learn how to walk, jump, and fly, and discover that your goal is to "move towards the light." Along the way you encounter obstacles, solve puzzles, discover bits of backstory, and run into other players in the desert. After completing the game, you're rewarded with an ambiguous, haunting ending, and then invited to play again so you can put your newfound knowledge to work by helping new players.

Journey creates a strong sense of place and reveals different experience layers upon replay. By modern gameplay standards, it's brief—you can complete the game in 2–4 hours. Yet playing and re-playing *Journey* is a deeply satisfying and powerful experience. Why? Because your transformation from newcomer to master is laid out with narrative artistry, and allows enough breathing room for your imagination.

We can't all create *Journey*-level game experiences, but we *can* be inspired by the artistry of great games. **The mastery path tool is designed to help you create an unfolding experience that adds up to a coherent and satisfying whole.**

So how do you create meaningful progression and make your customer the hero, whether or not you're building a game?

Skills, Knowledge, and Relationships

Start by identifying the skills they're developing, the knowledge they're acquiring, and the relationships they're building as they engage with your product. Each is a potential source of personal transformation.

These questions lay the groundwork for an experience that can engage your customers for weeks, months, even years. Ask yourself:

- What can my customers get better at that they care about?
- What skills do they develop when they engage with my product over time?
- What metric are they improving, and what makes that metric meaningful to them?
- What new powers, access, and privileges will open up as they progress?

For example, early on in Happify's development, we focused on moms who'd left the workforce and were highly motivated to improve their mood and overall well-being. Our goal was to teach them activities scientifically proven to raise happiness levels.

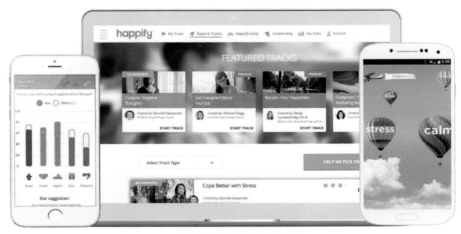

© 2018 Happify, happify.com

On the surface, these customers wanted to get better at being happy. Digging in, what they REALLY wanted was an easy, convenient way to boost their mood—both in the moment, and in the longer term. To accomplish this, we needed to help them form and stick to a "happiness habit" so they could reap long-term benefits from these proven activities. And that's what we did, using the mastery path to guide us.

Now it's your turn to learn this system and build deep engagement into your products from the ground up.

Discovery Is for "Visitors"

You never get a second chance to make a first impression. Your product experience starts with discovery—the moment when visitors first hear about your product through a friend, or via social media or advertising. That's when initial expectations are set and someone either is attracted by the idea and value proposition ("Sounds worth trying") or repelled ("Not for me—pass").

For discovery to be effective, it's vitally important to develop clear messaging about your core experience and value proposition. Your goal is to attract the right people, and to filter out those who aren't suited to or don't need or want your product.

The better you know who you're designing for, the more targeted your discovery messaging and acquisition funnel will be.

Sometimes, your customers will express their own take on your value proposition through word-of-mouth. If your product delivers on its promises, that's great news. For example, when I was heading overseas, several friends told me to check out Duolingo to pick up a new language. I decided to read App Store description and reviews—which confirmed the value proposition and general excellence of the product, so I downloaded it.

Write Your Discovery Story

Visitors are interested in personal fit. They're wondering: *Is this for me? Is this worth my time? What problem does it solve for me?* Your discovery story should answer these questions from a visitor's point of view.

Use this template to write a discovery story that captures your hypothesis about how your early market will discover, value, and check out your product.

Discovery story

WHEN I first hear about the product

I WANT TO understand the core value proposition (what's in it for me)

SO I CAN decide if it's worth checking out.

If you have more than one idea for a discovery story, great! Write them down. Your job is to **articulate your hypotheses**, and then gather data to update and refine them.

Onboarding Is for Newcomers

Onboarding is where visitors transform into newcomers. Think of onboarding as *"indoctrination of the initiates"*—people who have signed up and are eager to get value from the experience. Good onboarding invites them in, gets them engaged, and helps them learn the ropes.

What form should your onboarding take? That depends on your product, positioning, and goals. You can be brief and to the point like Duolingo, which gets people into the experience quickly.

Or you can be like Lumosity, a brain training service that engages you in a dialogue about your performance goals and current health habits during onboarding, then prescribes games that engage your sensory and cognitive systems.

Write Your Onboarding Story

Effective onboarding helps customers acquire knowledge and build their skills. It also sets their expectations about what's to come. Newcomers might wonder:

- How do things work here?

- How do I learn the ropes and start getting value?

- What's in this for me? Why should I invest my time?

Your onboarding story should answer these questions. Here's the template.

> ### Onboarding story
>
> **WHEN I** first join the system
>
> **I WANT TO** feel welcome, learn the ropes, and achieve small goals
>
> **SO I CAN** quickly get value from the experience.

If you know what your early adopters are looking for, you can write a solid onboarding story. If you're not sure, sketch out a story that articulates your best guess. In either case, you'll have a hypothesis that you can test and refine with real customers.

Habit-Building Is for Regulars

What does it take to turn an experience into a habit? For each of us, the answer is deeply personal. We become habitual users of games, apps, and services when they hit that a sweet spot of opportunity, need-fulfillment, and social context.

I use Twitter, for instance, as my proverbial water cooler during breaks from work because that habit fits my needs and lifestyle, and it helps me stay in touch with colleagues around the world. Contrast that with my daughter, who uses Musical.ly to share lip-syncing videos with her friends. Each product drives a powerful habit for some people—and not for others.

Turn Newcomers into Regulars with Product-Based Habit Stories

How do you turn a newcomer into a regular? By building a compelling habit. This might involve reading updates, meeting new challenges, or deepening personal connections. Now it's time to imagine what your core product habit could be. To do that, you'll write a **product-based habit story** that describes the ritual of using your product. The story involves repeatedly performing an engaging activity and getting a hit of satisfaction that keeps you coming back.

Identify Promising Insights from Your Research

Start by identifying promising habit stories from your research. Ask yourself:

- What existing need and/or habit could drive customers to use my product?

- What skill or competency will they build by using my product?

- Is there uncertainty or anxiety attached to NOT having that skill?

Answering these questions will help you create an experience that keeps your customers coming back. Here are a couple of habit story templates to get you started.

Habit story 1

WHEN I log in here regularly

I WANT TO see fresh content / activities / challenges / matches / people

SO I CAN get a "hit of satisfaction," AKA the outcome I want.

Sam Hulick on Upgrading User Skills

Samuel Hulick is a user onboarding expert who runs *useronboard.com*, where he deconstructs the initial experience of popular apps and services.

Daniel Cook's talks and articles showed me where product design and game design overlap. Games help users develop skills in the virtual world, while products help users develop skills in the real world.

When you approach product design as upgrading user skills and encouraging accomplishment, you take the natural motivation and energy that someone brings to an experience and use it to your advantage. Otherwise, you're trying constantly to steer people towards something that isn't aligned with what they're looking to do.

> ## Habit story 2
>
> **WHEN** I use this product regularly
>
> **I WANT TO** get better, more personalized recommendations and content
>
> **SO I CAN** get more value from my time investment.

Piggyback on Existing Habits

Designing your product experience around an existing habit is the surest way to drive uptake and adoption.

For example, our Pley customer research revealed a nightly video-watching habit among kids, plus a need among the parents for trusted, family-friendly content. This insight prompted a pivot in product strategy for the team, and saved them from building something nobody wanted or needed.

> **WHEN** I get the kids off to daycare and have a moment to myself
>
> **I WANT TO** look through beautiful images of a home life I aspire to
>
> **SO I CAN** feel inspired, and escape the drudgery of my daily routine.

Our Happify research revealed a daily habit of browsing Pinterest to transition after dropping off the kids. This insight prompted us to do a UX pivot from an isometric gaming display to a flat Pinterest-style feed filled with beautiful, inspiring images.

> **WHEN** I want to grab a few minutes to relax after my workday
>
> **I WANT TO** let my Lego-obsessed kid watch videos unsupervised
>
> **SO I CAN** relax guilt-free without worrying about inappropriate.

Mastery Is for "Experts"

Each year, our family makes its annual pilgrimage to Cazadero Family Performing Arts Camp, known as Caz. For one magical week, we leave our everyday selves behind, and become our camp selves.

At Caz, I'm "AJ the bassist," trudging through the woods, dragging my amp and my beloved Tobias Killer B bass guitar, supremely happy to be holding down the bottom end in the gospel, funk, and hip-hop classes.

Immersed in an Alternate, Simplified Reality

Going to Caz reminds me of what I love about the games: that feeling of being immersed in an alternate, simplified reality, a place where you can escape from your everyday life. I've had that sensation while playing so many games, but most deeply while playing MMOs. And like every great long-lived summer camp, MMOs have figured out how to keep their customers engaged over time.

- During **discovery**, you hear about amazing experiences people had, often from friends, and it sounds like a world you'd like to be part of.

- Once you arrive, you have fun and learn the ropes during **onboarding**, taking part in structured activities designed specifically for newcomers.

- You keep returning and make it a **habit** because you form relationships, collaborate to accomplish your goals, and find that greater challenges and learning opportunities appear as your skills develop.

- If you go deep and **master the system**, new roles open up that allow you to have greater status, rewards, and impact on the community.

New Opportunities for Leadership and Impact

Character transformation is compelling, and mastery opens up new opportunities for leadership and impact. One thing I love about Caz is watching kids grow into young adults and campers grow into staffers. My friend, Sarah Myers, for example, started as a camper and now teaches a popular mosaic class.

Like all well-run summer camps, there are many ways to peek behind the curtain and contribute to the experience. At Caz, campers with an artistic gift like Sarah often morph into teachers, staff, and volunteers. Last year, after attending for six years, I had my level-up moment: my Jazz teacher, Larry, asked me to sit in on his morning Hip Hop class to provide a steady, strong beat. I was thrilled to do it, because it meant he was bringing me behind the curtain and counting on me as a fellow musician.

Mastery Is Intrinsically Motivating

We know from self-determination theory—and our own experience—that competence and mastery are deeply, intrinsically rewarding. We also know that mastery doesn't come easy. It takes effort and self-transformation. That's what gives it meaning and satisfaction.

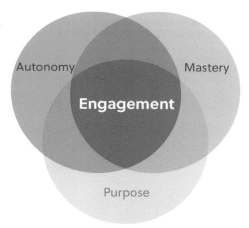

Games can tap into our desire to feel ourselves getting better at something. They give us an alternate, simplified reality—a micro-world— where we can immerse ourselves, learn the boundaries, master the rules, and visibly improve our skills.

A good game has the power to make us feel smart and competent, even when our world is falling apart. In contrast to the ups and downs of real life, the right game can reliably reward us for focused effort.

Mastery Is Better than Progress

Many non-game designers understand this and eagerly adopt points, badges, leaderboards, and ratings systems to track and reward progress. They soon learn what every game designer knows: **Numbers alone don't confer meaning.**

To create a compelling mastery system, your need context, challenge, and character transformation. Consider *World of Warcraft* (WoW). The motivational power of WoW's progression system isn't embodied in the points, levels, or milestones; those are scaffolding, like the framing of a house. WoW is compelling because of the story you tell yourself and the skills and relationships you develop, and because you gain new powers and take on new roles and challenges. For those who've earned it, there's nothing more motivating than a new, challenging role to play.

Outside of gaming, Slack is a great example. Slack is missing the cluttered-up game mechanics of so many engagement wannabe tools, and yet its path to mastery is incredibly effective. It's built around customization and the idea of integrating with an API. The way to get better at using Slack is by making it more and more your own, and by taking on larger challenges just like you might in a game. In customizing Slack and launching your own channel, programming a bot, and integrating your product into the Slack API, you travel Slack's path to mastery.

Give Your Best Customers an "Elder Game"

Not everyone needs to experience this path, but those who want to go deep can have more impact with the more they learn. The name for this? The elder game.

Imagine you're the director of a well-run, idealized summer camp that's secretly a role-playing game to empower learning and mastery. How would you describe the basic camp roles, rules and goals in gaming terms?

- **Campers** can participate in chosen activities and develop skills and character

- **Staff** (game-masters, counselors, teachers) are there to help campers develop their skills, find their passions, resolve disputes, and have a great time.

- **Rules** (have fun, be respectful, don't disrupt people's fun) are clear, visible, and easy to understand. People who break the rules don't get to play.

- **The campers' goal** is to have fun and develop their skills and character.

- **The staff's goal** is to create an experience that campers want to return to.

Some campers come once or twice and then decide it's not for them. Others—let's call them regulars—love the experience and return year after year. They're dedicated, focused, and sometimes a touch crazy. They develop their talents, master an activity, and max out their learning opportunities. In gaming terms, they're level-capped.

That's where an elder game comes in. It offers a new type of earned challenge or activity that wasn't available at lower levels. At our idealized summer camp, the elder game is to help run the camp, either as a staffer or volunteer. Enthusiastic campers get the opportunity to level-up and become counselors or teachers at their beloved camp.

Create Roles that Leverage Earned Skills and Knowledge

More than anything, experts want to show off their hard-won skills and knowledge. Depending on the game, you might create one or more of these elder game roles:

- **Champions** develop their talent, excel, and become stars and local celebrities.
- **Teachers** create and run programs and classes to help their students learn.
- **Greeters** help newcomers feel welcome and answer their questions.
- **Mentors** select promising newcomers and share knowledge and resources.
- **Game masters** keep the camp running and settle disputes.
- **Curators** spotlight excellence, judge contests, create playlists, mount shows.

To choose the right elder game role for your community, ask yourself:

- What skills, knowledge and relationships are experts accumulating?
- What kind of roles are experts asking for? What are they eager to do?
- What does the community staff currently do that could be handled by experts?

How can you keep your experts engaged and happy over time? The answers to these questions will guide you. And if you don't have any experts yet, don't worry. It's too early for your elder game. That can come later.

Create a "Forever Loop" to Keep Advanced Players Engaged

Once you've identified elder game roles, create a special mastery-level learning loop (described in the next chapter) with the potential to keep them engaged indefinitely. Make sure the central activity that drives your loop (plus any associated content) is both compelling and ongoing for these advanced players.

Out of necessity and resourcefulness, *Lineage* (an early Korean MMO) developed a "capture-the-flag" elder game. High-level players banded together and gained access to a different activity where they could raid a neighboring village, obtain the magical chalice, and then tax the citizenry.

If a group managed to do this, its own castle would become vulnerable, thus setting off the friendly "I'll get you back" competition that drives spectator sports and game tournaments.

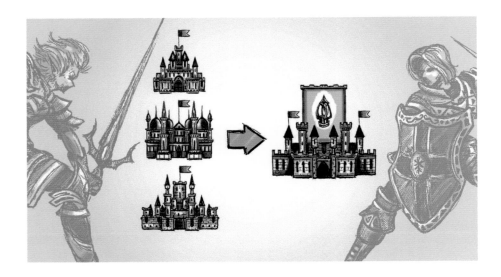

Empower Experts to Have Real Impact

When *League of Legends* became overrun with negative behavior and needed to scale player management operations, it created the Tribunal, trusted players empowered to triage abuse reports and settle the simple ones. These players are the first line of defense for internal customer support. They can rotate in and out of the role, which creates a forever loop for longtime experts who enjoy playing judge and jury.

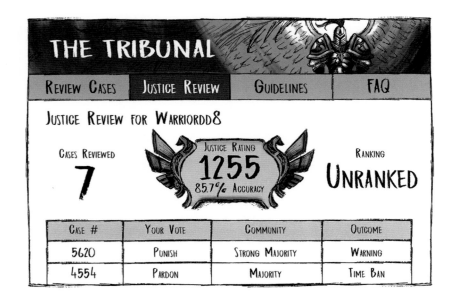

THE TRIBUNAL

| REVIEW CASES | JUSTICE REVIEW | GUIDELINES | FAQ |

JUSTICE REVIEW FOR WARRIORDD8

CASES REVIEWED
7

JUSTICE RATING
1255
85.7% ACCURACY

RANKING
UNRANKED

CASE #	YOUR VOTE	COMMUNITY	OUTCOME
5620	PUNISH	STRONG MAJORITY	WARNING
4554	PARDON	MAJORITY	TIME BAN

The most compelling reward for your investment is impact—not trinkets. If you're developing a community-based property, figure out how to empower passionate customers and give them a meaningful role in the system—one with the potential to transform their emotional state from "over it" to "into it."

Write a Compelling Mastery Story

Now that you understand how mastery works, it's time for you to write a mastery story for your situation. Imagine what types of experiences your most talented, dedicated customers might want. Some people want impact on the community; others care more about rewards, status, access, or an entirely new role to play. Here's the template.

Mastery story

WHEN I make the effort to master the system

I WANT TO earn powers, access, privileges, and rewards

SO I CAN stay engaged, challenged, and have an impact.

Co-create Mastery Systems with Superfans

At this stage, you won't know exactly what your mastery systems will look like. Nonetheless, go ahead and jot down a hypothesis for what mastery could look like in your system. Ask yourself: *What would motivate my best customers to stick around?* But don't spend too much time on it, because early on, you need to focus on bringing your core learning loop to life (coming up next in Chapter 7).

Once you connect with superfans, you'll funnel those insights into refining your hypothesis and building out your mastery systems—like we did with all the hits I've worked on (see Introduction for details).

On *Rock Band*, for example, our early superfans were rhythm-action gamers who were willing to come into the office during their lunch hour, week after week, and play rough early versions of our game. We tested and tuned our mastery systems with their input, going through many iterations that our mainstream customers never saw.

Worksheet: Mastery Path

Now it's your turn. Answer these questions to sketch your end-to-end customer experience.

Start with Customer Insights

List the most relevant job and habit stories from your customer research.

Discovery Story for Visitors

Write a discovery job story imagining how customers will first hear about your offering:

When I [first hear about or discover the product],

I want to [quickly understand the core value to me]

so I can [know right away if it's a good fit and worth checking out]

Onboarding Story for Newcomers

Write an onboarding job story imagining how potential customers will feel—and what they're looking for—when they first start using your offering:

When I [join the service/sign up for the app/try the product],

I want to [feel welcome and learn the ropes]

so I can [feel confident and quickly get value from the experience].

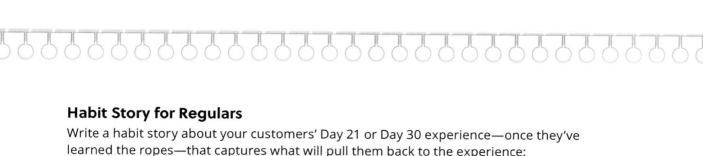

Habit Story for Regulars

Write a habit story about your customers' Day 21 or Day 30 experience—once they've learned the ropes—that captures what will pull them back to the experience:

> When I [come here regularly, e.g. the daily experience four weeks in],
>
> I want [fresh content, activities, or challenges]
>
> so I can [always get that quick "hit" of satisfaction I'm seeking].

_____

_____

_____

_____

Mastery Story for Experts

Write a mastery job story about what the experts experience a few weeks in. What experience/powers/rewards/role can you offer them that leverages the skills, relationships, and knowledge they've built up using your system?

> When I [make the effort to master this system],
>
> I want [earned unlocks, powers, access, status, roles]
>
> so I can [stay engaged/have an impact/leverage my newfound skills, knowledge, and relationships].

_____

_____

_____

_____

Mastery Path Speed Bumps

As you're crafting the customer's journey to mastery, don't let these speed bumps slow you down.

Speed bump #1: Little feedback from early customers

Customer feedback from your internal team, your investors, and your friends can skew your thinking. These people are not your early market. You need feedback from people who don't know you. Watch out: you may be building a house of cards and limiting your growth.

Take the time to find and learn from true early adopters. Make sure you're testing your product's value proposition with the right people. If your outreach channel isn't working, fix the problem and try again.

Speed bump #2: No support for skill-building

If your product is shallow or trivial, it can be tough to create a compelling customer journey. Without character transformation and skill-building, you can't lay out a compelling ascension path. And without that, the journey is a lot less satisfying and much easier to leave.

You need to **create a system that drives customer value over time.** Build and tune simple versions of you core value-building systems right from the start. Even in crude form, this will help test and develop your value proposition.

Speed bump #3: Not a coherent experience over time

Writing job stories will help you identify your product's through-line from your customer's point of view. If your stories are fragmented or inconsistent, that's a sign that you need to back up a few steps and rethink the experience.

To create a deeply engaging experience, **tighten your narrative into a compelling customer journey.** See if you can write job stories that hang together in a coherent whole. When you collect new insights, revisit your stories to refine your understanding and keep focused on what's most important to your customers.

Chapter 7

Design Your Learning Loop

In a loop, you're learning a skill and updating your mental model. That's what leads to player delight.

Dan Cook, Author, *Lost Garden* blog

I REMEMBER THE SINKING FEELING OF watching a brilliant entrepreneur get seduced by the siren song of onboarding. Against my advice, he created and shipped a beautiful, polished onboarding experience to get users into the system and "see what happens." But there was no compelling reason for users to return regularly.

Not surprisingly, that app was a leaky bucket; hardly anyone stayed around after downloading and trying it out. The developers did a great job with discovery and onboarding—but didn't invest in developing the habit-building phase of the experience.

Finding the Fun in Hit Games

What do the makers of breakout hits do differently than that well-meaning entrepreneur?

The *Rock Band* team kicked off the project by tuning the core dynamics of playing a single song, over and over again, and testing many different feedback systems until it felt like playing in a band.

The Sims team spent months building crude simulation prototypes to test out different versions of the core gameplay—many of which were dead ends.

The *Covet Fashion* team brought their cooperative game to life with iterative testing—and the end result looked very different to what we'd originally imagined.

Tinker, Prototype, and Playtest

All these successful innovations kicked off with an **experimental phase of tinkering, prototyping, and playtesting**. Great games and products aren't fully designed up-front, they're prototyped into existence, brought to life through iteration and tuning.

The best product leaders discover what works by relentlessly testing and tuning their ideas. In gaming, we call this "finding the fun" and "scoping." In Lean/Agile, we call it "customer development" and "validating assumptions."

All these terms point to the same fundamental activity: running experiments to test and tune your product idea and value proposition. That means you'll need to choose a specific part in your customer's journey to start prototyping and testing.

What's a Learning Loop?

The most successful product creators I know always kickoff a new project by building, iterating and tuning the core activity chain, or what I call the core learning loop. Once that's working well, they'll start to add more features and polish. If you want to emulate successful innovators, this is how you build engagement from the ground up.

So, what exactly is a learning loop?

Is It a Landing Page?

You might be thinking "Hey wait. Why should I invest in building an entire loop? Isn't the best MVP a fake landing page?"

Not always. A fake landing page tests your marketing message. It won't tell you anything at all about your product experience. In game thinking terms, you're testing the discovery phase of your customer's journey. When you're bringing an engaging idea to life, what you need to test is habit-building, and the core bit of value embedded in that repeatable, pleasurable activity you're going to deliver.

Is It a Habit Loop?

A habit loop, as popularly cited*, is an operant conditioning loop built around cues, routines, and rewards. Although it looks like a tempting solution, operant conditioning techniques will give you a short-term lift, but will never lead to player delight, deep learning, or true long-term engagement.

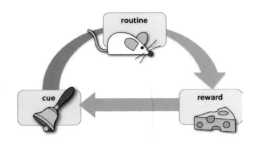

For that, you need skill-building, the exact thing that's missing from a habit loop.

Skill-Building Drives Reengagement

While an operant conditioning loop is focused on shaping behavior, a learning loop is focused on empowerment, helping your customer get better at something they care about. A learning loop has:

- A repeatable, pleasurable activity with internal triggers.

- Feedback that drives learning and skill-building.

- Progression and investment with reengagement triggers.

In *Rock Band* (or when playing real instruments), the learning loop elements are:

- The repeatable, pleasurable activity of playing music, triggered by a desire to play music, and the drive to get better at your instrument.

- Feedback from listeners, peers, and teachers that drives learning and improvement.

- Progression and investment in instruments, practicing, and technique, with triggers that urge you to keep playing and getting better.

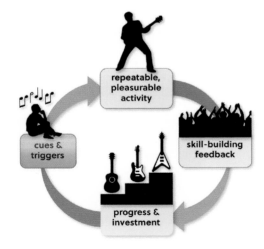

In strategy games like *Clash of Clans*, the loop systems can get more complex. This game has a nested loop structure that revolves around building and training troops, collecting resources, and battling enemies.

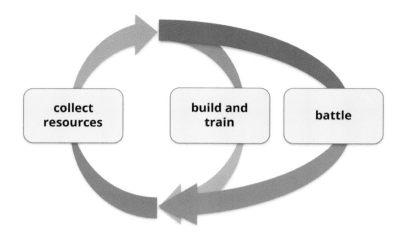

Don't let this scare you. It's not always so complex. Some highly effective gaming loops have just a few activities that work together to offer a rich and satisfying experience.

For example, the *Bejeweled* learning loop is quite simple: Solve match-three puzzles (a repeatable, pleasurable activity with simple feedback) to level up (progress) and earn new powers (investment).

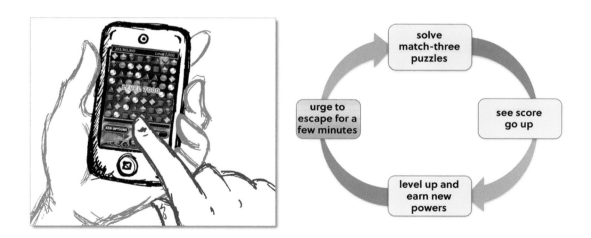

Mike Sellers on Systems Thinking

Mike is a game designer who helped create *Meridian 59*, the first graphical MMO (massively multiplayer online game). He now teaches game design at Indiana University.

Systems thinking is to the 21st century what literacy was to the 20th century. Early in the 20th century you could get by without having to read or write. But eventually it became a necessity for living in our society.

Most people don't understand what systems thinking is. The truth is, you will need it to operate effectively in the 21st century. Games give us a powerful way to model and learn about systems such as climate change and the global economy.

In a non-gaming context, SnapChat has developed a compelling learning loop with simple feedback that tells you how many people have read your stories and what percentage of your content those people have read. This feedback, coupled with SnapChat's daily filter changes and disappearing messages, creates something people find irresistible.

Repeatable, Pleasurable Activities Fuel the Loop

Activities are the atomic units of engagement. Without something engaging to do, people won't keep coming back to your product in the long run.

A simple, effective learning loop starts with a repeatable, pleasurable activity that's connected to an internal and/or situational trigger.

In *Rock Band*, the core activity is playing a song with your friends, and the internal trigger is the urge to do something fun together when your friends come over to hang out. In *Candy Crush*, the core activity is solving match-three puzzles, and the internal urge is distracting yourself with just one more level. The pleasure in these activities is amplified (but not determined) by the surrounding context, both the underlying systems and the visible environment.

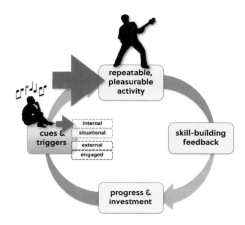

To create a stripped-down MVP, ***find the pleasurable, repeatable activity at the heart of your product experience.*** You may not have progress markers or social feedback in your earliest prototypes, but you *will* need some pleasurable, repeatable activity for customers to do. Here are some examples outside of games:

- **YouTube:** watching videos

- **Kickstarter:** checking out campaigns that you care about

- **Twitter:** reading and responding to updates and messages

- **Duolingo:** play a language-learning mini-game

Feedback Makes Learning More Fun

When you're first bringing a game to life, "finding the fun" usually involves delivering some form of simple feedback. **Feedback is more fundamental and pervasive than progression.** Games use feedback loops; so do web and mobile apps.

The right feedback at the right time can induce that magical flow state we talked about earlier. If you've ever played *Dance Central*, *Rock Band*, or *Guitar Hero*, you've experienced immersive, skill-building feedback. Playing those games is like having a great coach whispering in your ear, helping you learn from your mistakes and try again. The feedback is that good.

Feedback alone can have a powerful effect on behavior. Just consider the real-time speed-display signs that are becoming more popular on roadways. Recent studies showed that these signs are far more effective than photo-radar for getting people to slow down.

You're on the Right Track, Baby

As you're building your MVP, make sure to include feedback that tells your customers they're on the right track. Slack, for example, offers light, charming visuals that confirm you've read all your messages—the core activity in the system.

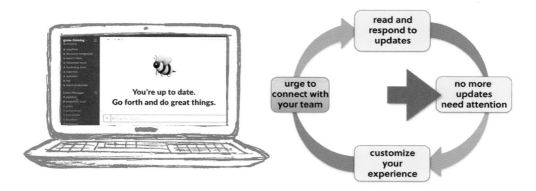

Progress and Investment Pull People Back

Sports, martial arts, computer games, and formal education are all systems built around structured progression and learning. A strong, well-designed progression system can enhance learning and motivation, and make it more fun and rewarding to improve your skills. Progress markers can drive reengagement and enhance your customer's experience.

Activities and feedback work together to engage your customers and let them know they're on the right track. **Investment** is what happens when you collect, earn, customize, win, or build something you don't want to lose. **Triggers** are reminders to return to the system you're invested in. Together, all these techniques pull your customers back and complete your core learning loop. Let's dig deeper into how these interlocking concepts work.

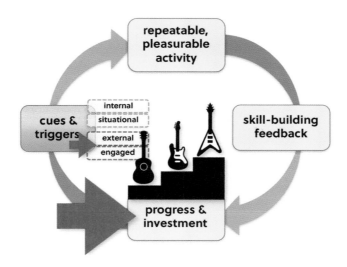

Investment Makes It Harder to Leave

Anytime you create an avatar, refine your profile, check your stats, earn points, integrate your address book, post an update, or curate your friend list, you're deepening your investment in that system, and making it harder to leave. There are many ways to invoke feelings of investment in your customers. Here are a few.

Stats worth checking: Self-improvement is a powerful force. It's inherently motivating to see yourself getting better, stronger, faster, smarter, or more popular. That's why so many systems tune their tracking algorithms to show visible progress, it gets people hooked and keeps them coming back. A simple example is Twitter's follower count, which engages you in growing your audience, which makes it harder to walk away.

Tell me a story: People love to tell and listen to stories. Anytime you get your customers to tell you a story about their experience—or even better, share that story with other customers—you're driving investment. Stories can take many forms, such as updating Instagram, posting to a forum, or leaving a comment on a blog.

Enhance my self-image: Anytime you customize your identity or environment, you're investing a bit of yourself into the system. If you purchase new running shoes, you're enhancing your self-image as a runner, and investing money into the habit. When your customer chooses colors, selects a background image, or creates an avatar, they are increasing their investment in your system through personal expression.

Help me connect with people: Some people thrive on social motivation and engagement. If you're that type of person, you'll feel more invested in something if you can share it with others. The exercise app Endomondo, for example, offers an easy way to build your friend network and share your workouts. If your friends are holding you accountable, it's harder to drop out.

Currency is for spending: Once customers are engaged with your system, giving them spendable currency is a powerful way to drive investment. This tactic is most effective if it's layered onto other skill-building systems, instead of being used in isolation. Duolingo, for example, awards "lingots" for completing activities, which you can spend on customizing your profile.

Triggers Remind You to Do Something

Triggers are internal or external events that remind you to *do* something. Triggers come in four distinct flavors, and often combine and blend together to drive behavior.

Customer-centric triggers already exist in your customer's experience. You learn about them through discovery research.

- **Internal triggers** are emotions, urges, or cravings your customer has, such as hunger, loneliness, excitement, anticipation, curiosity, boredom, etc.

- **Situational triggers** are transitions, rituals, and events that occur regularly, such as waking up, commuting to work, or sitting down for family dinner.

Raph Koster on Core Loops

Game designer Raph Koster helped design seminal MMOs like *Ultima Online* and *Star Wars: Galaxies*. His book *A Theory of Fun* connects games and learning.

When I design an original game, I start by prototyping the core mechanic. Does the core loop have enough depth so that as players keep discovering new things as they play? Is the game presenting the player with the information they need make decisions and master the system?

That core learning loop is something that I try to work through in the prototype. However, I'm often not right. I'm only one player.

So I test the game with other people. After they've played it, I ask them "What were the things that made you feel excited? What were the things that frustrated you? What were the things that you wished you could do but you couldn't?"

I'm looking to find the emotional connection they have with the game.

Product-centric triggers are designed into your product experience. The most effective ones tap into the customer's existing emotions and habits.

- **External triggers** are environmental cues that remind you to do something, such as notifications, email, shoes by the door, or sticky notes on your laptop.

- **Engaged triggers** kick in once someone is engaged in your experience. If you have an internal urge supported with external feedback, that's an engaged trigger. Checking your stats in a game or your unread messages in Slack are two good examples of triggers that kick in once you're engaged in the system.

Imagine that your goal is to exercise more often. How would different types of triggers help you accomplish this?

- After a stressful day, you might feel an urge to work out. Scheduling your workout to coincide with this craving is motivated by an **internal trigger**.

- If you stop at the gym on your way home from work, you're piggybacking your workout onto a repeating **situational trigger**—driving home from work.

- If you leave your workout clothes on the front seat of your car to remind you to stop by the gym, you're using an **external trigger** to encourage workouts.

- If you join a 30-day group countdown, and check your stats to see how you're doing in comparison with the rest of the group, you've got an **engaged trigger**.

How to Design Your Core Learning Loop

Now that you've learned the basics, it's time to design a learning loop of your own.

Leverage Your Job Stories

Start with **relevant stories** from your customer research that combine an **existing habit with an unmet need**. For example, Pley translated a video-watching story into a simple learning loop—built as a YouTube channel for their high-learning MVP.

Let's take a look at the elements in that loop.

- **Internal trigger**: Parent needs free time, wants a "benevolent babysitter."

- **Repeatable, pleasurable activity**: Watch a Lego-related instructional video.

- **Feedback**: Customers can express their preferences via comments and ratings, and Pley-run contests helped get customers to submit videos.

- **Progress, investment and engaged triggers**: Social media updates when new videos are released, and customers share their favorites.

Look for Emotional and Situational Triggers

As you've sifting through your job stories, look for emotional and situational triggers that prime customers for using your product. Understanding these triggers will help you identify existing habits—like these triggers we surfaced during our Pley research:

- I want some guilt-free time to myself (immediate need).

- I want to develop my kid's creativity (longer-term need).

- Dinner is over and I need to do the dishes (immediate need).

- I wish my kid could build more structures with this set (longer-term need).

The frazzled parents we interviewed didn't want a mindless video babysitter, they wanted their kids to be inspired. So Pley built a loop that engages kids, and then equips them to go back into the world to build something creative. To identify existing triggers for your product, ask yourself:

- In which situations is my customer most likely to seek out my product?

- What's happening right before—and after—those moments? What's the context?

- How does my customer *feel* right before—and after—using my product?

- What pain or itch does my product alleviate? Which emotions are driving use?

Answering these questions will help you design a product that hooks into your customer's context, internal state, and existing triggers. And that's a great starting point for driving adoption, satisfaction, and long-term engagement.

Build Your Prototype Around Engaging Activities

Engaging, repeatable activities are the atomic units of your core learning loop. When you're setting out to build your MVP, start by creating a simple, stripped-down loop around your key activity. If you can create a repeatable, pleasurable activity that your customers want to get better at, you've laid the foundation for habit-building and long-term engagement. Getting that core activity loop tested and working is what we call "find the fun" in game design. Building your MVP around this activity loop is the best way to **build engagement from the ground up.**

Sometimes, this activity might not be what you first set out to build. For example, we hypothesized that our Pley customers would want to participate in a conversational online community. But our discovery interviews revealed that our superfans wanted family-friendly Lego videos to keep their kids engaged—something they couldn't find elsewhere.

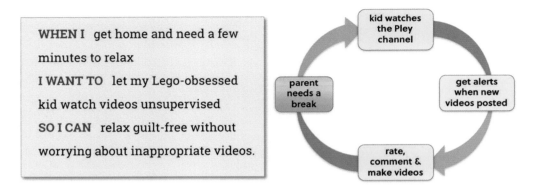

To test our idea quickly, we created a YouTube channel and filled it with educational Lego videos by and for kids. This activity loop let us test the value of delivering targeted video content to their customers, before investing in building our own infrastructure.

Motivate Skill-Building with Simple, Compelling Feedback

As you're bringing your product to life, ask yourself: ***What feedback would help my customers perform their core activity better?*** When we think of games, we often focus on visible progression systems like points, badges, levels and leaderboards.

Yet feedback is more fundamental than progress. Feedback lets you know you're on the right track and motivates you to stay engaged in what you're doing.

Consider *Minecraft*. Right from the start, *Minecraft* had direct visual feedback for building, breaking, and mining with blocks, like a crude **digital Lego set**. You could create simple structures and show them off by calling someone over to your screen. No progress bars, no points or lives—just feedback.

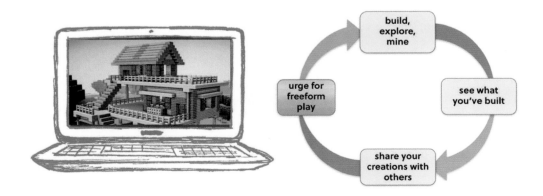

At this stage of development, *Minecraft* was more of a simulation demo than a game. What was always present was real-time, compelling visual feedback. The developers never embraced the structured progression systems that many hit games depend on, and yet their game became a massive worldwide hit.

We Love to Watch Numbers Going Up

We humans sure love to watch numbers go up, don't we? Social networks like Twitter, Facebook, LinkedIn give you social feedback with a collecting mechanism. Likes, comments, shares, ratings, and subscriptions—that's what those numbers represent. Watching your stats grow creates a feedback loop built around personal progress and comparing your stats to others can lead to friendly (and not-so-friendly) competition.

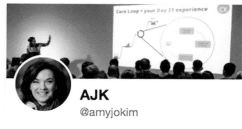

What's missing is a mechanism that ties these stats into meaningful unlocks and progressive skill-building. How would *you* answer these questions?

- When a customer uses your product for months, what are they getting better at?

- How will you show personal or social progress in a compelling, meaningful way?

- How is your customer's Day 30 experience different or better than Day 1, or Day 7?

- Once someone learns the basics, which features, content or access can they unlock?

You don't need to have detailed answers to these questions right now. The point is to start thinking about the core systems you'll build to evolve your customer's experience over time.

Worksheet: Learning Loop

Now it's your turn. Answer these questions to design your core learning loop.

Start with Habit Stories

List the most promising habit stories from your customer research, using this format:
When I [come here regularly], I want [fresh XYZ] so I can [get that quick "hit" of satisfaction].

Identify Internal and Situational Triggers

Look through your habit stories and identify the emotions and context that trigger the habitual behavior. What could drive your customers to seek out your offering? What situation could remind your customers to return again and again? Write down the internal and situational triggers you know about (or need to validate).

Design Short, Pleasurable, Repeatable Activities

Write down the simplest version of a pleasurable, repeatable core activity or chain of activities that customers will experience during a typical product session.

Design Feedback to Motivate Skill-Building

Write down the simplest bare-bones feedback your product can offer to help customers know they're on the right track.

Drive Investment and Progress

Write down the stats, stories, customization, collections, and other mechanisms that will drive deeper engagement and motivate return visits. What kind of progress or investment systems are already familiar to your customers?

Pull People Back with External and Engaged Triggers

Write down ideas for the external triggers—email, notifications, etc.—you might use to pull customers back. How does that trigger fit into your customers' existing habits?

Also write down ideas for the engaged triggers—stats, dashboard, unread updates, etc.— you might use to encourage regulars to return. Why are these effective triggers for your particular customers and situation?

Learning Loop Speed Bumps

As you're designing your core learning loop, watch out for these common speed bumps.

Speed bump #1: Unappealing or boring activity

Pleasure matters. It's tough to build a sustainable core learning loop around an unappealing or boring activity. If the basic actions at the heart of your system are unappealing or boring, it'll be tough to sustain interest, no matter how much fluff you put around it.

If you run into this problem, spend some time up front to **refine your core activities and make sure they're pleasurable and repeatable.** That will create a foundation you can build on.

Speed bump #2: Relying on extrinsic motivators

If your core learning loop design relies too much on extrinsic rewards and motivators, you may be able to drive short-term engagement, but your house of cards will be likely to crumble.

Make sure your design is compelling because of the core activities, not just the progress mechanics, rewards, or notifications. If you develop engaging activities and a strong value proposition, you'll be set up to drive sustained engagement.

Speed bump #3: Forgetting to close the loop

I've worked with many startups and game studios who can create a compelling activity, but have a hard time with driving reengagement. Extrinsic motivators can help, but only in the short term. If you can't find a way to drive deeper investment in your system, it'll be tough to get people to reengage in the long term.

Think about what skill, knowledge, or relationships your customers are building and **design reminders that tap into your customer's deepening investment** in your system.

Chapter 8

Map Out Your Social Actions

In a multiplayer game, the people playing are more valuable than all the animations, models and game logic.

Gabe Newell, CEO of Valve

WHEN YOU'RE BRINGING YOUR IDEA to life and building your MVP, you need to put aside your grand visions and focus in on just a few core activities. Gaining that clarity and focus can be tough. Many entrepreneurs over-build their MVP because they don't know how to strip down their design, and they don't have the confidence, tools and guidance to make those hard choices and limit the activities they implement for their MVP.

As you know, **repeatable, pleasurable activities are the beating heart of your learning loop.** You're now going to learn a technique for identifying the social activities that best support your learning loop and map to your customers' needs and desires. This set of activities will define your product's social engagement style, and will you map build a stripped-down, high-learning MVP.

Systems Explain the World in Simplified Form

What's your guilty pleasure? Mine is taking those pop-culture personality quizzes that show up whenever there's a new hit movie, game, or TV show. I know these quizzes are over-simplified and silly, yet I can't resist answering a few questions and discovering who I resemble, and how my character fits into the larger scheme of humanity.

We humans love to create systems that explain the world in a simplified form. Back in ancient Greece, doctors based their treatments around the four temperaments: sanguine (sociable and pleasure-seeking), choleric (ambitious and leader-like), melancholic (analytical and literal), and phlegmatic (relaxed and thoughtful). The ancient Ayurvedic medical practice of balancing Doshas—Vata, Pitta, and Kapha—is based on similar groupings of human body/mind types.

The Four Temperaments

Choleric   *Sanguine*   *Phlegmatic*   *Melancholic*

Player Types in Social Gaming

Our medical practices have evolved, yet these basic human archetypes remain relevant. In the business world, we have Merrill's social styles and the DISC leadership model—systems targeted at helping diverse teams work together. In literature, we have the Hogwarts sorting hat, an oracle that places new students into a social group that matches their character. In pop culture, we have Rubin's character index, an analysis of how different people respond to rules and expectations.

In social gaming, we have Bartle's player types: achiever, explorer, socializer, and killer. Richard Bartle, an early MUD developer, noticed that certain social patterns emerged in a variety of game settings. He described these patterns as player types, and laid out an analytic framework for thinking about online social behavior.

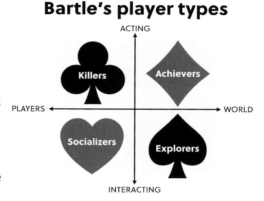

Personality systems embody the wisdom of "different strokes for different folks" in a simplified form, and give us a common language for discussing human behavior.

The Problem with Player Types

Like many game designers, I've used Bartle's player types to guide my work in MMOs and online competitive games. Bartle's system is great for raising awareness that **different people enjoy different types of fun**.

Yet, when I've tried to apply Bartle's system to casual, social and educational games, it wasn't a good fit. For example, when I was building games for a high-traffic women's portal, we found that the "killer" archetype was non-existent in their player base. Apparently teenage male hackers don't want to hang out on a website full of moms.

Things get tricky when you take a model developed for one purpose and context, and transplant it elsewhere. How far can you extrapolate social patterns from one situation to another? How can you discern if the model offers valuable insight, or leads you astray? How do you know if you've got the right categorization model for your project?

Start by asking a few clarifying questions about any model you're considering:

What's the purpose of the model? What aspects of human nature does it capture?

All categorization systems are designed for a specific purpose and context. Merrill's social styles and the DISC model help people with disparate styles work together successfully. Rubin's character index describes how individuals respond to rules and expectations. Bartle's player types describe social patterns that arise in multiplayer combat-based games. When considering a categorization system, look for its original purpose and context. That will help you decide if it's a match for your needs.

How does that match up with the activities and affordances in YOUR system?

Take a look at the structure and activities within your system. If it's people working together in teams, then the DISC or social styles could be a useful analytic tool. If your experience is fundamentally single-player or solo, then social models won't work, but Rubin's character index could be useful if, for example, you're creating a habit-building product and dealing with how people personally respond to rules. I found that Bartle's model works well for multiplayer social games like MMOs, MOBAs, and arena shooters, but less well for casual games, educational games, and health games.

Does the model explain emergent behavior you've already observed?

The most important test for a categorization system is whether it explains the patterns you've already observed. If you've found a system that maps well, go ahead and use that as your starting point. Don't be afraid to tweak and change it to better match your unique situation. For example, after running into problems applying Bartle's player types, I tweaked the model to better explain common behavior and motivations I was seeing. That updated model, called Kim's social action matrix, has proven to be far more useful for the lightweight social experiences and games I focus on.

Kim's Social Action Matrix

Inspired by Bartle, I took my experience with designing social games and identified four actions, or verbs, that emerge in online environments: compete, collaborate, explore, and express.

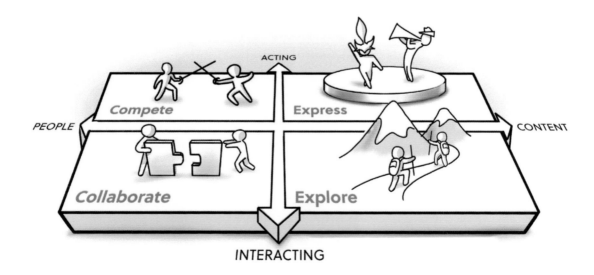

Richard Garriott on Player Types

Richard Garriott is a pioneering game designer, second generation astronaut, and creator of *Ultima Online*, the first popular graphical MMO.

Any online community includes all four Bartles player types. So, In Ultima Online, we included features that allowed you to steal, pick pockets, and attack other players.

To balance the game, we made a rule that you couldn't attack other players in towns, but you could attack in the woods. We intended that if you were a blacksmith in town you might need to hire miners to go to the caves out of town and bring back iron ore, creating an economic loop between two different types of players.

But people found ways to game the system to take advantage of other players. An expert player would say "I see you're a beginner. Come with me into the woods and I'll show you how to hunt." Once out of town, they would attack the beginner and steal their belongings. Our challenge became: How do we make the world exciting for hunters, without destroying the fun for beginners?

Compete

This is the urge to test your skills and see how you stack up. Competitors find ranking systems and zero-sum mechanics appealing, because those structures mirror their internal dialogue and POV. They love to showcase their prowess and know where they stand within a group. They seek mastery, learning, and relationship-building via friendly competition.

Collaborate

The urge to work with others toward a shared goal. Collaborators love the feeling of "winning together." They enjoy forming partnerships, participating in groups and teams, and playing co-op games. They value teamwork, shared learning, and relationship-building.

Explore

This is the urge to gain knowledge, explore boundaries, find loopholes, and know the rules that govern a space. Explorers love to poke at systems and discover their ins and outs. They enjoy accumulating and showing off knowledge. Explorers value accurate info, clever design, and relationship-building via knowledge exchange. They can enjoy exploring with others, but often, it's a satisfying solitary endeavor.

Express

This is the urge toward self-expression and a hunger to personalize their experience, make their mark, and express their uniqueness. They'll fully use any available tools to make things that others admire and emulate. They value original thought, creativity, hard work, and personal style. They enjoy customizing backgrounds, fonts, and avatars. They seek status, recognition and influence through creative skill.

Social Actions vs Player Types

Why make this shift? Why not just stick with player types? I've tried both and found that, when teams build a social action matrix, several good things happen:

- Once you remove the need to lump players into a limited number of categories, you open up the opportunity to create unique clusters of actions that describe the particular motivation of your players. This process is inherently more flexible than archetypes and leads to actionable output.

- Your team focuses on the actions people take and the motivation behind those actions. This mapping makes it easier to translate unmet user needs (uncovered during customer discovery) into systems, features and UI affordances.

- Once your team has a tool to rank and prioritize social actions, they're more effective at triaging and prioritizing bug fixes and new features throughout the product life cycle.

- Once you visualize and identify the core social actions in your product, your team is better equipped to identify and focus on core social and progression systems. Not every team is good at systems thinking, so I embrace any tool that helps teams develop this crucial skill.

This simple, practical tool will help you recognize and design for common motivational patterns. I've used it during product strategy, feature planning, and user experience debugging, with great results. I find social actions to be easier to map onto product design than player types—just like job stories are easier to map than personas.

Who Are Your Customers? What's Their Social Engagement Style?

Once you know your hot-core audience, use the social action matrix as an analytic tool. What motivates your audience? What's missing from their lives? What qualities reinforce their identity and tap into an aspirational view of themselves? Are they competitive or collaborative? Involved in self-expression or exploration? Here are some common actions mapped against the four quadrants. Which of these actions can your customers do in your product experience? Map those out, and you'll see your social engagement style.

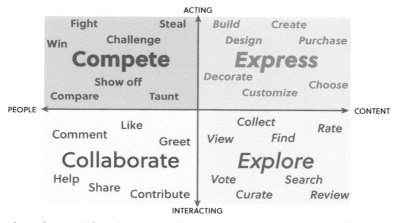

Let's take a look at the social actions in Kickstarter. This popular crowdfunding service plays to our aspirational desire to be patrons of the arts and support projects and people we believe in.

KICKSTARTER Social action matrix

Matt Leacock on Cooperative Games

Matt Leacock is a board game designer and UX expert. His first hit game, *Pandemic*, is a cooperative board game where players team up to save the world from virulent diseases.

My wife and I played a negotiation board game and it got really nasty. We both finished the game and felt horrible, and wondered why we had done that. Then we tried "Lord of the Rings", a cooperative game where we played together against a common foe. Even when we lost we both felt really, really good.

I thought the design was interesting, and I wanted to see if I could make something similar. That led me to create "Pandemic," a game I would enjoy playing with her.

I've been able to use my entire UX design toolkit in my game design work. One thing I love about user experience design is paper prototyping—being able to quickly create a design, get feedback, and iterate it.

With board games, the paper prototype IS the product. I don't need someone else to code it. Tweaking the game is as easy as pulling out a card or crossing something out and rewriting it.

With an ever-growing variety of projects, Kickstarter is a gold mine for **explorers**, and the multi-tiered investment structure enables **collaboration** with a few clicks. You can see which friends backed a project, but not how much they contributed, which minimizes competition.

Now let's look at Happify, the popular mental health app.

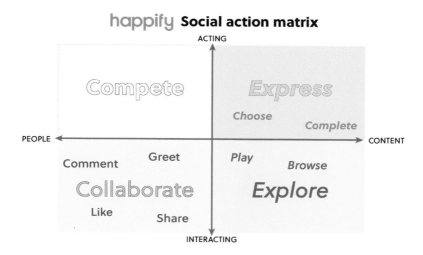

Notice that Happify's social engagement style is similar to Kickstarter: heavy on collaboration and exploration, with a bit of self-expression.

Neither app enables direct head-to-head competition—something that competitive games excel in.

Contrast the feeling and style of interaction in Kickstarter and Happify with the popular mobile game *HQ Trivia*. There, the verbs cluster into the compete and express quadrants, with a bit of collaboration that happens through sharing and helping.

There is no right or wrong answer to your social engagement style question. What's important is to focus on the quadrants that best match what your customers are looking for from your experience. This is especially helpful when you're building a stripped-down MVP or alpha test.

How to Create Your Own Social Action Matrix

Let's say you've just done some customer development research and gained a better understanding of your customers' needs, habits, and motivations. You and your team are now fleshing out and prototyping your ideas.

Use the social action matrix to assess the alignment between what you want to build, and what your customers care about. Start with a blank social action matrix:

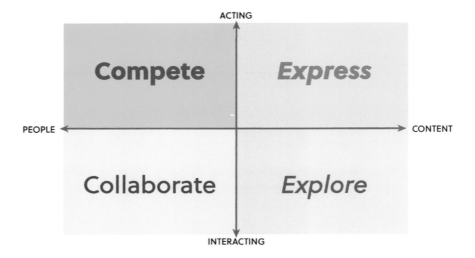

In COLOR 1, write the social actions that your product enables. Place those actions on the matrix where they most align. In COLOR 2, write the social actions that represent your customers' unmet needs and core motivations. Place those on the matrix as well.

Now step back and ask yourself: **how does your product align with the needs and motivations of your customers?** If it does align, double-down on your efforts. If it doesn't, you have work to do—either in retargeting your audience, or rethinking your design.

No model offers the ultimate solution. Think of the social action matrix as a starting point for understanding what motivates your players, and use it to focus on the most important social actions to include in your MVP or alpha test. Once you understand how it works. don't be afraid to tweak it to capture your audience and application more closely—just like I tweaked Bartle's model to come up with this.

Worksheet: Social Action Matrix

Now it's your turn. Answer these questions to fill out your Social Action Matrix.

Compete

What actions might your customers take to compete with each other, showcase their prowess, or participate in ranked competitions?

Collaborate

What actions might your customers take to collaborate, form partnerships, or participate in groups or teams with shared goals?

Express

What actions might your customers take to express themselves, personalize their experience, or show off their unique creative skills?

Explore

What actions might your customers take to explore boundaries, discover what is possible, or possibly show off their knowledge?

Social Action Speed Bumps

As you're mapping out your social actions, watch out for these common speed bumps.

Speed bump #1: Trying to populate all quadrants

Successful products usually start with a limited set of actions that delight early customers and then grow from there. Don't try to populate all the quadrants in your matrix—that's not the point of this exercise. Trying to provide multiple actions for every social style is a common mistake that will prevent you from focusing on what matters most.

To avoid this problem, try to **focus on the two quadrants that map best to your customer's motivation.** Write down the actions that your product enables in those quadrants. If your product's actions are distributed in all the quadrants, you may have a focus problem. Consider cutting back on your feature set and building a more streamlined experience.

Speed bump #2: Confusing progress with competition

Everyone loves to make personal progress towards their goals—that's human nature. When it comes to interacting with others, some people enjoy the thrill of head-to-head competition, while others prefer to band together, cooperate, and beat the system. When you're mapping out your social actions, make sure not to confuse personal progress (e.g. earning points and levels) with social competition (e.g. leaderboards). They're very different activities, driven by different motivations.

You can avoid this confusion by using the mastery path tool (Chapter 6) along with job stories (Chapter 5) to **map out your customers' personal progression path.** From there, think carefully about what kind of social engagement would motivate your customers. Don't assume that everyone loves to compete. While leaderboards and head-to-head battles can be highly motivating for some people, others are put off by zero-sum mechanics and prefer "winning together" within cooperative play.

SECTION IV
Playtest

It's what we think we know that keeps us from learning.
Claude Bernard, Physician

Early prototyping and testing are central to design thinking, and the lean startup movement embraces high-learning experiments and building an MVP, or Minimum Viable Product. We know that to increase our odds of success, it's smart to test product ideas early with the right people. But too many people end up testing their solution hypothesis too late in development.

In Section II, you learned how to find your superfans and synthesize relevant insights from their experience. In Section III you learned how to design a compelling customer journey and core product experience.

Now comes the payoff—the stage where you leverage all your hard work and run product experiments with hot-core early customers. In this section, you'll learn how to create the right artifact or prototype for testing, and run high-value playtests that answer your questions and guide your team towards success.

Chapter 9

Prototype Your Core Activity

MVP is a liquid, not a solid.

Steve Vassallo

A FEW YEARS AGO, I LED some projects for a fast-growing crowd-funding platform. One was focused on adding a complex and strategically important feature—international shipping—to our platform. As we evaluated wireframes and mock-ups, I made plans to bring in a few power users to look over our flows. But my plans were derailed by pushback from management. ***"That's not how we do things here. We don't show unfinished work to customers."***

So no early validation and testing for us. Instead, we simply built what the internal team "knew" was right and released this much-requested feature a few months later. Guess what happened. The power users—the ones who needed it most, the ones who jumped on it first—*hated* the design because it didn't match their mental model of the task. We scrambled to fix the problem, sucking up dozens of hours of engineering, design, and product management time.

Get Actionable Feedback on Your High-Risk Assumptions

This story illustrates exactly why you want to test your assumptions up front. For the crowd-funding platform, our high-risk assumption was that ***customers will think about this complex feature in the same way we do.***

This assumption turned out to be false, and the fix was costlier and more time-intensive than testing the idea early with a few well-chosen customers.

If you develop a habit of testing early and often, with the right people, you'll avoid this costly mistake and save yourself time in the long run. And it all starts by creating the right artifact to test. Whatever form your prototype takes, remember that your goal is to get as much actionable feedback on your high-risk assumptions as possible. Here are some guidelines to keep you focused and productive during prototyping.

Prototype Your Core Activity, Not Your Marketing Message.

Make sure that your team knows the difference between product discovery and product experience. A landing page will test your marketing message, but it's a waste of time if what you really need is to validate your core product experience and value proposition.

Embrace a "Good Enough" Visual Aesthetic You Can Update Quickly.

To maximize learning, build mock-ups that are *good enough* to test and learn from. Leverage your early adopters; they don't need fancy visuals to offer useful feedback. The faster you update, the more you'll learn and the more likely you'll be to succeed.

Use Prototyping Tools to Quickly Bring Ideas to Life.

Find the quickest, simplest way to visualize and test your ideas. Resist the urge to over-engineer; leverage prototyping tools, off-the-shelf solutions, and rough mock-ups.

Choose the Right Artifact to Test.

An effective prototype can take many forms. You can productively test:

- a **competitor's product** that you want to understand better.

- a **scenario walk-through**, illustrated with sketches, mock-ups, or wireframes.

- **clickable mock-ups** (built with a prototyping tool) with which someone interacts.

- a **simple working prototype**, website, or crude early version of a game.

- a **hardware prototype** that your subjects can touch and interact with.

You can learn valuable lessons testing any of these forms. Which is the right one for you? It depends on your product complexity, development stage, and skill set.

Sketches and Scenarios

If you're early in the design process, you may have sketches, wireframes, or mock-ups of your ideas. Now, not everyone has the imagination to look at low-fidelity visuals and envision what they might become. However, some early adopters *can* give you useful feedback, especially if you bring those visuals to life with a narrative about how the product might work.

When to Test Scenarios

If you want early customer feedback on a product idea, UI flow, or progression system, testing low-fidelity visuals can be highly instructive and can save you time and headaches down the road. To get useful feedback from low-fidelity visuals:

- Select the right testers (early adopters, power-users, etc.).

- Setup the visuals properly (see testing protocols in Chapter 10).

- Test early enough for the results to shape your product/UI/progression system.

When Not to Test Scenarios

If your core experience truly depends on polished visuals, it will be tough to get actionable customer feedback without it. And if your team and stakeholders don't trust research insights from rough scenarios, you'll have a hard time making product decisions with this technique. In those situations, scenarios are not the best choice.

Tracy Fullerton on Prototyping

Tracy Fullerton runs the trend-setting USC Game Innovation Lab. Her most recent game, *Walden*, puts the player inside Thoreau's Walden Pond experiment.

One of your first tasks as a game designer is to find a group of core players. Once a week or so, test a new iteration of your idea.

The iterations don't have to be very deep. They can be storyboards. They can be paper prototypes. You don't have to spend a lot of money. In fact, you can do a much broader exploration if you make five quick paper prototypes, throw three away, then take good ideas from the other two into the next iteration.

Make sure you have a revolving door of the kind of users that you need for playtests. We've been designing educational games, so we put together a group of teachers who like what we're doing. When we need to test a game idea we invite kids to come in and play a card game.

Cheap, fast iteration is powerful because you fall in love with your own idea if you spend too much time articulating it.

Clickable Mock-Ups

A great way to visualize and test your core learning loop is with a few clickable mock-ups of key pages and flows. Many product creators use prototyping tools like Keynote, Invision, or Balsamiq to quickly mock up and test different versions of their product. This is a great way to iterate quickly and test different ideas without much engineering investment.

When to Test Clickable Mock-Ups

Clickable mock-ups are great for getting feedback on your UX flow, screen design, and details like navigation, naming, and layout. Just know that as soon as you show customers something specific, they will react strongly. So keep your graphics as simple as possible and focus their attention on the elements you need feedback on.

When Not to Test Clickable Mock-Ups

If you don't have a clear idea of your product focus, clickable mock-ups won't solve your problem and they might even send you down the wrong path. In that case, it's better to create sketches and walk your subjects through a day-in-the-life scenario.

Working Prototype, Game, or App

It's always great to test a working prototype of your core functionality on early adopters. If you're further along, you can use all these techniques to collect customer insights on your working product and plan an effective pilot/beta test. If you're building a game, you're probably focused on getting a rough prototype working, tested, and iterated as quickly as possible. It might be a paper mock-up, or a working demo (created with prototyping tools like Unity or GameMaker). Testing the rules and core activities will tell you how close you are to "finding the fun."

Wizard of Oz/Concierge Test

Is it possible to create a high-learning prototype quickly, with little or no engineering? The answer is yes, if you're building an application where it makes sense to test your core business hypotheses by using humans to simulate what will eventually be automated components.

A manual-first test of your value proposition is called a "Wizard of Oz" test (if the humans are hidden) or a "Concierge" test (if the humans are visible). This can be a highly effective way to connect with your early customers and find out what they want, before you've invested heavily in engineering. Airbnb and Aardvark are two famous service-based apps that started as manual-first MVPs.

Once you've clarified your hypotheses with the MVP canvas, it's worth considering if a manual-first MVP could help you test and refine your assumptions. Just don't force it—this approach is not for everyone. For example, many digital games aren't amenable to this approach, but most services and marketplaces are.

Hardware Prototype

If you're developing hardware, a manual-first MVP probably won't cut it. You need to build something that your potential customers can pick up and handle.

Your first prototype will likely be cobbled together with spare parts and duct tape, which will help you iterate quickly. That's a great place to start. From there, you can build and test progressively more developed versions of your product, like the iterations of Google Glass shown here.

Competitive Products Are Your Secret Weapon

If you're not ready to show your sketches, mock-ups, or prototypes to your early adopters, try running playtests using a competitor's product. For example, if you're working on a social sharing product, you could recruit teen girls to use Snapchat and debrief about how they utilize it.

This technique is a goldmine; you learn how your customers think and talk about issues in your market space, and sharpen your testing skills along the way.

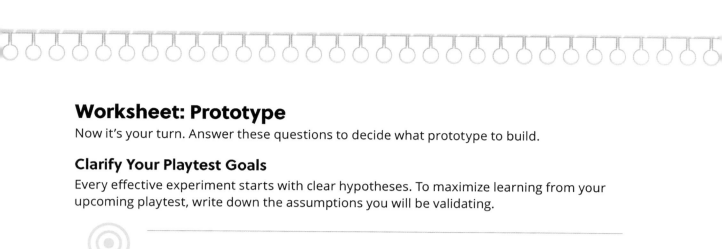

Worksheet: Prototype

Now it's your turn. Answer these questions to decide what prototype to build.

Clarify Your Playtest Goals

Every effective experiment starts with clear hypotheses. To maximize learning from your upcoming playtest, write down the assumptions you will be validating.

Choose a Prototype Format

Select the prototype format you will use at this stage of development.

- Sketches or static mockups
- Interactive mockups (computer, phone, tablet)
- Paper prototype (mostly for gaming)
- Hardware prototype
- Simple, stripped-down working game, website, or system
- Concierge/Wizard-of-Oz service

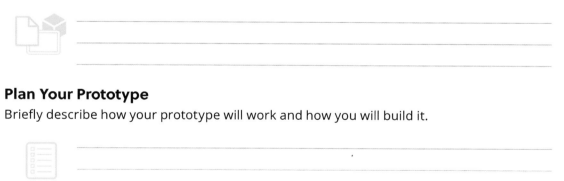

Plan Your Prototype

Briefly describe how your prototype will work and how you will build it.

Prototyping Speed Bumps

As you prototype your core activity, watch out for these speed bumps along the way.

Speed bump #1: Focusing on discovery or onboarding

There are many ways to make an MVP. Popular solutions like creating a fake landing page test discovery, but can be distracting and misleading.

Make sure your team knows the difference between testing product discovery and prototyping your core product experience and value proposition. To build an engaging experience, **focus on testing and tuning your learning loop first.**

Speed bump #2: UX and graphics perfectionism

Watch out for the lure of visual quality and polish. There's a time and place for that in product development. During early prototyping, polishing your graphics and UX will slow you down dramatically.

To maximize your learning, move fast, leverage your early adopters, and **build interfaces that are "good enough" to test and learn from.**

Speed bump #3: Over-engineering your prototype

Similarly, resist the urge to over-engineer your prototype. This isn't the time to build scalable code; it's time to iterate fast and cheaply, with as little code as possible.

Find the **quickest, simplest way to mock-up your ideas for testing.** Whenever you can, use prototyping tools, off-the-shelf solutions, and hacked-together mock-ups.

Chapter 10

Test Your Idea with Hot-core Customers

You can use an eraser on the drafting table, or a sledge hammer on the construction site.

Frank Lloyd Wright, Architect

Plan Your High-Learning Playtest

It's critical to choose the right people for testing low-fidelity versions of your product.

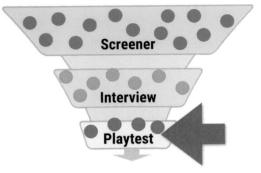

Earlier, you identified a handful of potential MVP testers using the superfan screener and speed interviews.

Now it's time to setup and run short, high-value testing sessions with these hot-core early adopters.

Schedule One-Hour Testing Sessions

It can take effort and energy to coordinate calendars, so start scheduling your testing sessions as soon as possible. In general, try to allocate one hour per session. This will give you enough time to interview your subject, test your prototype, and debrief.

However, if your prototype is simple and/or you're early in the process, you can get tremendous value from a half-hour session. Use your judgement and schedule sessions that fit your needs and your subject's availability.

Paid or Unpaid?

If you're building an app, product, or game that's aimed at consumers, you will probably want to pay your subjects. A good default rate is $50/hour, but I've paid anywhere from $25 to $100 for a one-hour interview, depending on the age group, income level, and expertise level of the participants. To keep things simple, we offer subjects an Amazon gift certificate as payment, or a certificate to their favorite store.

If you're targeting enterprise customers, it may not make sense to pay your subjects. In some situations, it might even violate professional protocols. Instead, try to set up 30- or 60-minute "informational interviews" with potential superfans and to get their feedback on your value prop. Think about something you could offer them other than payment in return for their time.

Solo or Pairs?

By default, most people think of user testing as a solo activity and will schedule one person at a time for sessions. If your product is likely to be used solo—without social interaction—this is a good approach, because you're reproducing your core use case.

If your product will likely be used in a social or family setting, where multiple people might be interacting, watching, or commenting, you'll get better, more actionable data by scheduling pairs or small groups of subjects.

Pair Testing Reveals Thought Processes and Social Dynamics

Pair testing can be especially valuable for surfacing people's thought processes, because your subjects will naturally talk to each other as they interact. To get the most from these sessions, try to reproduce the social setting of your core use case. If you're not sure, schedule a few tests with solo subjects and a few with pairs, then evaluate which approach delivered better results and do more of that.

Local or Remote?

It's often useful to see people face-to-face so you get the opportunity to read their body language (as well as listen to their responses). If your subjects are local, you can increase your learning bandwidth by running testing sessions in person. For example, you can set up a simple "testing lab" in an office or conference room as Google Ventures does, and invite subjects to a series of interviews.

Alternatively, you can meet people at their homes, or at public meeting places like bars or coffee shops and conduct the interviews there.

This is a higher-overhead approach, but potentially more revealing and useful for data collection. It's okay to be experimental and opportunistic. If this seems a like promising idea, try it out and see what you get.

You can also run your sessions online, using video-conferencing software like Skype or Zoom. If that person is in the setting where they'd use your product, these remote sessions can be especially useful. For the Pley interviews, for example, we used Skype to interview parents and kids about their Lego habits, right in their home environment.

Write Your Three-Part Playtest Guide

To get most out of these sessions, use this three-part structure to guide your time.

Part 1: Warm-Up

In the first part, you'll get to know you customer better and set them at ease. Which questions should you use to open the testing session? That depends on what you've already learned about these people during your screening survey and speed interviews.

Follow up and go deeper

When speed interviews go well, those short conversations leave you wanting more. Now is the time to follow up on the most fruitful questions from those interviews, and dig deeper into any relevant issues, emotions and habits you're curious about. And because this is a natural continuation of your earlier conversation, it can help put your subject at ease.

Introductory interview, if needed

Sometimes, you want to test someone who did not go through your two-stage filter, and so never went through that initial speed interview. In that case, simply create an introductory interview for this testing session, using the templates and instructions from Chapter 3.

Transition to show-and-tell

It's good to develop a habit of testing early and often. So whatever stage you're at, think about what you could show your early adopters in order to test your hypotheses. Ease into it. After you warm-up interview, tell them you're shifting gears, and that now you'd like to get their reactions to a product concept that's related to your conversation.

Eric Zimmerman on Play Testing

A self-described playtest fundamentalist, Eric designs games that explore new forms of play on and off the computer, and is a professor at the NYU Game Center.

I believe that play-testing as early as you can is the key to game design. People entering the industry for the first time often think that the concept behind the game is the main thing. Once you have the concept, executing the game is just a matter of crossing your T's and dotting your I's.

That couldn't be further from the truth. Actual design happens once you start building the game and play-testing it.

One of the pleasures of play-testing is seeing all of your brilliant ideas shattered on the rocks of reality. If I have a group of students arguing about whose idea is better, I say, "Everyone go make a prototype. Come back here in 15 minutes and we'll try them out."

I teach game design off the computer—everything is a tabletop, physical, or social game—so people can quickly prototype and iterate ideas. That's harder to do once you move to a digital medium.

Part 2: Test

Next, you'll show them your prototype or product (in whatever form), let them interact with it, and notice their reactions. This might be:

- a competitor's product (to get insights into your market).

- an early hardware prototype (duct tape and components).

- a playable paper or physical mock-up.

- a working prototype of a website, app, or game.

- clickable mock-ups, sketches and wireframes.

Give them tasks and ask them to "think aloud"

The ideal way to run a playtest is to give people a challenge and watch them figure it out. Try to create tasks for your customer that test your assumptions. For example, if you're building a video app for kids, you might ask kids to launch the app, find a video they like, and start playing it. If your prototype or product is far enough along, you can instruct your subjects to perform the tasks, then watch and learn as they stumble through it and voice their questions.

For earlier-stage products, you can get value by asking how they would imagine performing a certain task using your product and then listening carefully to the language they use to describe that activity. Scenarios are great for this stage.

Just before you run the test, instruct them to "think aloud" and say whatever runs through their mind If you're testing in pairs, you have an advantage because they'll naturally talk to each other. All you need to do is get them started and listen in.

Part 3: Debrief

After your subject has seen and interacted with your prototype, you'll spend a few minutes debriefing them to capture their reactions and feelings. A good way to ease into this transition is to ask a question along these lines:

"Now that you've tried it out, how would you see this product fitting into your life?"

Ask in a neutral way, so they feel comfortable with being honest, and letting you know if it does *not* really fit into their life. That's valuable to know!

Once they're eased into the debrief period, follow with these questions, customized to fit your needs.

Question 1: Habits and Triggers

When would you see yourself wanting to use this product? What time of day? What location? What would you be doing beforehand, and right afterwards?

Find out how your subject sees the product fitting into their life. Dig into the habits and situational triggers that could push them to use it.

Question 2: Likes and Dislikes

What did you like most about this experience? And what didn't you like? There are no right or wrong answers. We want your blunt, honest opinion.

Find out what they liked best about the experience and, even more importantly, what they didn't like. Get details. See if you can understand why they feel the way they do.

Question 3: What I'd Improve

What would improve the experience for you? If you could wave a magic wand, what would you love to see that would really impact your experience and make your life better?

Ask what they'd improve about the experience. Take note of any products or services they compare to your product experience—that tells you how they're positioning your product in their mind.

Run Your Playtest

Once your testers are scheduled, your prototype is prepped, and your interview script is written, it's time to run your experiment and start collecting data.

Use Interviewer/Notetaker Pairs

You'll get more out of these sessions if you run them with a colleague. Have one person conduct the interview and guide the subject through the testing session while the other takes notes and identifies emergent patterns. For best results, switch roles so that everyone gets a chance to be both interviewer and notetaker. It's more fun that way, and you'll get better data with more eyes and ears processing it.

Interviewer   Subject

Notetaker

Dress to Put Your Customers at Ease

Consider who you'll be speaking with in your interviews and try to dress in a way that builds empathy. Whether you're interviewing office workers in suits, rebellious teens in sandals, or parents on the playground, dress as similarly as you can to your subjects. It will help them feel at ease and make it easier to connect.

This is especially true if you'll be interviewing people in person, but it goes for online interviews as well. What you're wearing and how you present yourself can dramatically affect how your subject responds to you—both online and offline.

If you're testing remotely, use video during the warm-up interview and debrief session of your playtest, and possibly during testing as well. When you can see their body language and facial expressions, you'll get much better information about your customer's true opinions.

Plus, if there are multiple people involved in your test—say, a parent and child, or two friends—you can watch their interactions with each other, which can be a gold mine of useful insights.

Summarize Your Results

Once you've run your playtests, get together with your team and summarize 3–5 actionable findings or patterns that are tied to your MVP canvas. Ask yourself:

What were the key findings? What did these people like and dislike?

Start by sifting through the data and noting the top 3–5 patterns from your sessions, paying particular attention to habits, ideas, and unmet needs that surfaced. When possible, match up each pattern with a quote (or paraphrase) from the subjects.

Which hypotheses did you validate? Which ones need revising/revisiting?

Which ideas or assumptions from your MVP canvas did this playtest validate with positive feedback? What does that tell you about their needs, habits, and desires? Now, ask yourself: Which of my hypotheses were invalidated by this test? Which ones need revising and/or tweaking? Why? Did the playtesters have a different take on the issue than I'd imagined? Was there an issue with language? Positioning? Dig into the details.

What were the most surprising things you learned?

If you're surprised by your findings, pay attention! That's learning in action. Take note of ideas and insights from your research that were unexpected and relevant. What surprised you? How does this impact your thinking going forward? During our Pley research, for instance, we learned that parents want instructional videos for each Lego set they rented. This insight motivated our content marketing team to bump the priority of making these videos—a tactical insight that paid off big-time.

After Playtesting, Reflect and Validate

Once you've synthesized your results, you're ready to update your product strategy and design. It's pivot or persevere time, and this juncture can be tricky to navigate. How do you translate results from your playtest into product design decisions? In your journey from problem space to solution space, this is convergence. In Section V, everything you've learned will come together to turn research results into product decisions. You'll learn how to update your product strategy and design with the game thinking tool kit, and set yourself and your team up for success.

Worksheet: Playtest

Now it's your turn. Answer these questions to plan your playtest.

Warm-Up Interview Script

A brief warm-up interview puts your tester at ease and gives you insight into their habits and needs. Write your warm-up script, using the following format:

> Tell me more about your experiences with [relevant activity] (follow-up questions from speed interviews).

> Now you're going to [describe upcoming test activities].

> What we need is honest input, so tell us what's going through your head, good or bad.

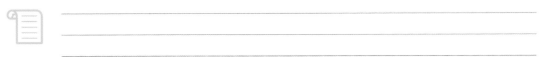

Session Plan

Write down your testing plan. How will you run your MVP tests? Solo or in groups? Remote or on-site? Who will be involved? How will you record it—with note-taking, audio, or video?

Playtesting Script

Your testing script tells subjects what to do as they interact with your product—without leading them to conclusions or biasing the results. It's helpful to write the exact words the moderator should say, so they don't have to improvise during the playtest. Your playtest script should include initial instructions, tasks the subject will perform, and scripted responses to common problems or questions that may arise.

Summarize Your Findings

What were the key findings from your sessions? Try to identify at least three patterns you saw across subjects.

What did your initial ideas/hypotheses were validated? What did testers like/love/get excited about?

What did testers dislike or respond poorly to? Which ideas/hypotheses need revising, tweaking, or more data?

What were the most surprising things you learned? Write down at least one response or finding you didn't expect.

Playtesting Speed Bumps

As you test your early ideas, watch out for these speed bumps along the way.

Speed bump #1: Putting words in their mouths

During the interview, your job is to understand your test subject's mental model and opinions. It's tempting to jump in and put words in their mouth. RESIST. Once you start doing that, you've changed the conversation and stopped collecting useful data.

Ask questions and give your subjects tasks, then sit back and notice the words they use to describe the experience. Don't correct them. **Just listen and take notes.**

Speed bump #2: False positives

While you may be a charming person (and I'm sure you are!), beware of charming your subjects. This leads to false positives. The surest way to undermine your experiment is to get your subjects saying what they think you want to hear.

To get honest, actionable feedback, **keep your language neutral and polite**, and make sure you welcome both negative and positive feedback.

Speed bump #3: Lukewarm response

It's disheartening to discover that your brilliant idea doesn't have legs. The longer you wait to discover this, the greater your sunk costs—all those hours, dollars, and dreams invested in chasing that vision. This is an "Emperor has no value proposition" moment—and in this moment, you have to make choice: embrace reality, or dismiss the results of customer discovery and keep on truckin'. Which do you think is most likely to lead to success?

If your testers were lukewarm, you have a problem. You want to see strong emotions, people leaning forward (literally or figuratively). Those are the signals that let you know you're onto something.

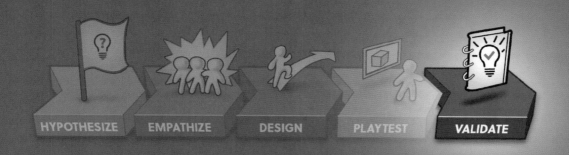

SECTION V
Validate

I tore myself away from the safe comfort of certainties through my love for truth—and truth rewarded me.

Simone de Beauvoir

Now that you've tested your core product experience with superfans, it's time to reflect on what you've learned and decide what to do next.

In this section, you'll learn how to update your product design and strategy with your newfound insights, to create a rollout plan that builds a compelling product experience, and guide your team's development efforts.

Remember back in Chapter 2, when you drafted your product brief? You're going to update that document with your newfound clarity and use the game thinking road map to map your customer's journey to your software release cycles. These tools will set you up to have productive conversations with your team and stakeholders, and make smart decisions about whether to pivot or persevere.

Chapter 11

Update Your Product Strategy

We are trying to prove ourselves wrong as quickly as possible, because only in that way can we find progress.

Richard Feynman, Physicist

AT THE BEGINNING OF YOUR GAME THINKING JOURNEY, you articulated your key assumptions and drafted your product brief. You then connected with early customers, surfaced their habits and needs, and used those insights to design and test your ideas.

Now it's time to use those results to validate your assumptions, update your strategy, and plan some new experiments. You know more than you did before so, in the language of stage-gate theory, you'll be placing your bets on the strongest ideas.

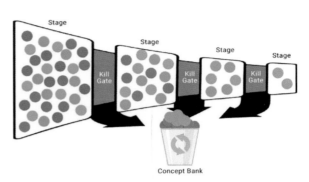

These customer insights might support your assumptions, or they might contradict them. Perhaps you uncovered something surprising or counterintuitive. Your job is to distill down all that input and decide what to do next.

Distill and Prioritize Your Research Results

At this point, you might be wondering, **"Which issues should I focus on? Which ideas should I pursue? If there's a conflict, who should I listen to?"**

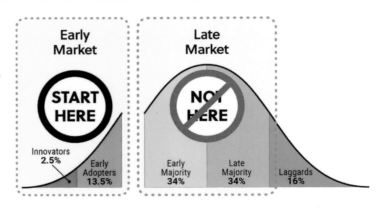

To help you sort through this, let's revisit our old friend, innovation diffusion theory. Each person who gave you feedback—coworker, investor, research subject, friend—falls into one of five buckets in relation to your product. As you're prioritizing your results, **focus on your early adopters**, the people who are excited to get their hands on what you're offering and will put up with pain and friction to get it.

Ignore the early majority naysayers; don't let them throw you off track. If you're doing something innovative, your job is to find and delight your early market, not to impress your boss, mom, co-worker, or hotshot friend.

Product Strategy: What We're Building

Once you've synthesized your playtest results, it's time to update your elevator pitch and MVP canvas to reflect what you learned. Think of this as a before-and-after product strategy "makeover" to update and improve your initial assumptions.

To do the makeover, follow these four steps:

1. Update what you know now about **early customers and unmet needs**. Were your assumptions valid? Invalid? Partly right? Capture your learnings.

2. Update your ideas about the **solution and value proposition** that connects to that need. How did your original ideas play? Were your assumptions valid?

3. Check for consistency with your **unfair advantage and early metrics**. Does the solution play to your strengths? Need to update metrics?

4. Finally, update your **key assumptions**—the ones you created and tested. You'll validate or invalidate them, and then generate *new* assumptions to test.

Elevator Pitch

We are building [your product concept in a nutshell]

for [your high-need, hot-core customers]

so they can [scratch an itch, fulfill a desire, target a pain point]

EARLY CUSTOMERS	UNMET NEED	OUR SOLUTION	UNFAIR ADVANTAGE	KEY ASSUMPTIONS
Not your ultimate larger audience, but who you will contact, design for, and sell to first.	Why do customers need your product? What problem does it solve?	What is your solution? How does this solve the customer's problem?	How is your company uniquely well suited to win?	What high-risk assumptions will you be testing as you build your MVP?
	VALUE PROPOSITION Why will customers prefer your product over competing products? What's different and high-value?		**EARLY METRICS** What will you measure to determine if your early prototyping efforts are successful?	

Customer Insights: What We're Learning

Earlier in Chapter 2, you drafted your initial research plan. Now, you'll update that draft and summarize your research process and key findings.

> ### Research plan
>
> **WHO:** [XX] people with [YY] characteristics.
>
> **WHAT:** early interviews or playtests designed to test [Assumption 1]
>
> **WHEN:** [XX] days from gating event.
>
> **WHERE:** [geographic location: online, in-person, etc.]
>
> **WHY:** tune our core systems, get early feedback on our direction.

Pivot or Persevere: What to Build Next

Finally, you'll update your team and stakeholders on what you want to do and build next, given what you've learned. Are you going to double-down on your current direction? Or make a substantial change?

Cindy Alvarez on Talking to Stakeholders

Cindy Alvarez, author of *Lean Customer Development*, is a principal researcher for Microsoft's developer division, where she tackles open-ended customer opportunities and drives internal cultural change.

Qualitative information will never be quantitative. Don't say "87% of people"—that's putting math clothes on qualitative research.

Instead, tell a story. "Here's a pattern we've been seeing. We've talked to a variety of people in a variety of industries and they all have this problem and here's how we know they have this problem. Here's how we've tried to disprove that they have a different problem. Here are a couple of solutions that might address that problem."

It's a story. It's open-ended. It suggests something actionable, but it's not dictating numbers, because no one likes that. Stories are what people remember.

Plan Your Alpha Test

The answer depends on whether you proved or disproved the assumptions you've been testing. For example, your answer may be to run an alpha test (or other kind of test) with your superfans for a number of weeks. If so, you'll want to sketch out who you'll recruit to participate, how long you'll run the test, and what you hope to learn.

Alpha research plan

WHO: [XX] people with [YY] characteristics .

WHAT: an [X]-week Alpha test designed to test [Assumptions 1, 2, 3]

WHEN: [XX] days from [gating event]

WHERE: [geographic location: online, in-person, etc.]

WHY: get early feedback on our core systems and features.

You'll also want to sketch out what you want to build for this test and what hypotheses you'll be testing. You'll also want to focus on tuning the learning loop in these early tests—something we'll discuss in detail in Chapter 12.

Turning Research Results into Product Concepts

Take a look at this "makeover" of our *Covet Fashion* MVP canvas. We used game thinking to test our idea for a F2P (free-to-play) cooperative game tied to real-world fashion trends. Our assumptions revolved around the premise of blending real-world fashion cycles with a F2P mobile game. Were fashionistas longing to play this type of game? Should we partner with a celebrity stylist?

What Stayed the Same: Unmet Need, Value Proposition, and Solution

The unmet need is a hunger for aspirational dress-up with high-end designer brands and real-world tie-ins.

The value-prop was "a *Vogue* replacement"—something beautiful and immersive that keeps you up-to-date on fashion trends. We thought our existing hardcore fashion-gaming audience would be our early customers.

Crowdstar's unfair advantage was its extensive F2F (face-to-face) experience, and an addressable audience for testing and marketing the game. Early metrics were drawn from subjective responses during weekly interviews over several months.

What Changed: Target Audience and Core Mechanics

After testing, we learned that our paying audience skewed older than we'd thought, and that some players didn't want to listen to a celebrity stylist, but rather wanted to *be* the stylist. Our testing showed that Crowdstar guessed right: testers love playing with real-world fashion.

This learn/measure/build cycle validated our solution and value prop in a few short weeks, allowing us to update our design ideas with useful tweaks. Based on this early validation, Crowdstar green-lit the team to develop the game further, and it went on to become the studio's biggest hit.

COVET Before

EARLY CUSTOMERS	UNMET NEED	OUR SOLUTION	UNFAIR ADVANTAGE	KEY ASSUMPTIONS
Young women 18–30 who play mobile fashion games.	Aspirational dress-up in designer fashions, plus advice from a celebrity stylist.	Free-to-play co-op game with real-world fashion content and hot trends.	Experience building free-to-play games. Existing, addressable audience for fashion games.	Young women want a mobile game based on real-world fashion. Young women want a celebrity stylist.
	VALUE PROPOSITION Stay up to date on fashion by playing, not just looking—AKA Vogue replacement.		**EARLY METRICS** Like/dislike metrics via interviews, with hard-core fashion gamers.	

COVET After

EARLY CUSTOMERS	UNMET NEED	OUR SOLUTION	UNFAIR ADVANTAGE	KEY ASSUMPTIONS
Young women 18–30 who play mobile fashion games. PLUS 30-45: older women also like the game and spend more.	Aspirational dress-up in designer fashions. PLUS advice from wanna-be stylists.	Free-to-play co-op game with real-world fashion content and hot trends.	Experience building free-to-play games. Existing, addressable audience for fashion games.	Young women want a mobile game based on real-world fashion, and will spend money in a real-world fashion game. Young women want a celebrity stylist — AND other up-and-coming stylists.
	VALUE PROPOSITION Stay up to date on fashion by playing, not just looking — potential Vogue replacement.		**EARLY METRICS** Like/dislike metrics via interviews, with hard-core fashion gamers.	

Pattern #1: The Fashion Browser

> **WHEN I** get home after a long day at work
> **I WANT TO** kick off my heels and relax, looking at high-fashion outfits
> **SO I CAN** stay up to date on the latest fashions.

Product Concept: Fashion Feed with Voting Game

Around 70% of our test subjects love to relax at the end of their workday by browsing up-to-date fashion content and commentary. We knew we needed something relaxing and easy to browse through.

From our research, we knew that these fashionistas considered their after-work browsing time to be educational, and would love a fun and interactive way to stay up to date on the latest fashions.

For these Coveters, the team designed an always-changing fashion feed to showcase the outfits players create plus a simple two-choice game to generate ratings on each outfit. This concept delivers what fashionistas care about: gorgeous, up-to-date outfits made from the latest designer fashions. And we deliver that in a fun, lightweight entertaining system, where the players entertain each other with their creativity, passion, and flair.

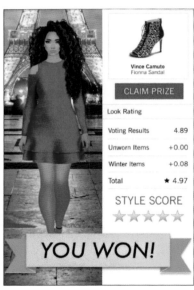

© 2018 Crowdstar, crowdstar.com

Steve Portigal on Checking your World View

Steve Portigal is a world-class expert in customer research and author of *Interviewing Users*, a practical handbook on how to get the most value from customer interviews.

The making-of video for "We Are the World" showed all these pop stars coming into a studio. Quincy Jones, the producer, put a sign up that said "Check your egos at the door," because so many big personalities were coming in to collaborate.

That's what I was channeling when I said, "Check your world view at the door." If you're going to enter someone else's environment and sit with them as they make travel reservations, or whatever activity they're doing, don't think about yourself. That gets in the way.

For customer interviews, you need to set your world view aside, and make sure you are ready to pick up on whatever is going on.

Pattern #2: The Co-Creator

One play pattern we surfaced is the co-creator, who loves to dress, shop, and primp with a buddy, usually a close friend or relative.

WHEN I need to dress for an important event

I WANT TO raid my friend's closet and get her advice on my outfit

SO I CAN have her accessorize my look and help me feel confident.

Product Concept: Shared Closet

Earlier in the project, we'd thought about squad-based cooperative challenges and came up with some compelling ideas. This pattern gave us inspiration for a much simpler cooperative play concept: The Shared Closet.

Just like in real life, you can raid your friend's closet and borrow her things if you're friends in the game. This creates an incentive to build your friend network, because it expands your wardrobe and chances of putting together a winning outfit.

This system also reproduces the real-world dynamic of "dressing together" with your best buddies to boost your confidence and morale. When you borrow something from a friend, she'll get updates about your outfit and can play along.

© 2018 Crowdstar, crowdstar.com

Pattern #3: The Armchair Stylist

Another common pattern we surfaced was the armchair stylist, who's highly opinionated about fashion and loves to tell *other* people how to dress.

> **WHEN I** give fashion feedback to others
>
> **I WANT TO** know that my feedback had an effect
>
> **SO I CAN** feel useful and important because I'm helping others.

Product Concept: Crowdsourced Rating System

This builds on the two-choice fashion game from Pattern 1. This rating system collects all the votes and gives feedback to the creators about how your outfit was rated.

Everyone gets feedback and a style score, framed in a positive way. But some people—the ones whose outfits get the most positive votes—get top ratings and special in-game rewards and prizes, including free virtual clothing and accessories.

This is an armchair stylist's dream come true; a way to sit at home (or take a break during the workday) and share your opinions about how other people are dressed. Plus, she can show off her style by playing to win, and collecting votes on her own outfits.

© 2018 Crowdstar, crowdstar.com

Worksheet: Product Brief (updated)

Now it's your turn. Update your product brief based on the results of your playtest.

Update Your Elevator Pitch and MVP Canvas

Look at your original elevator pitch and write a new version that reflects what you learned in your playtest.

Document Job Story–Customer Quote Pairs

Summarize and support your research findings by pairing job or habit stories with customer quotes (or quote synopses) that led to those stories.

Update Your Mastery Path

Write the updated job stories for discovery, onboarding, habits, and mastery.

Update Your Core Loop

Write down your revised ideas for triggers, repeatable activities, feedback, and progression.

_____
_____
_____
_____
_____
_____

Plan Your Alpha Test

Write a plan for your alpha test. What assumptions will you be testing?

_____
_____
_____
_____
_____
_____

Product Validation Speed Bumps

Look out for these common speed bumps when you're validating your product strategy.

Speed bump #1: Scope creep

Watch out for the natural tendency to expand your scope and broaden your goals—especially if you got confirmation on your product ideas from early customers. Even when thinking big, you still need to be disciplined and focused to iterate quickly.

Make sure your pilot project is small, focused, and streamlined. Be disciplined and clear about what you need to learn in order to move ahead.

Speed bump #2: Lost in the details

Your project brief is a summary of actionable, relevant info—NOT an exhaustive list of every detail you've heard and learned. Too much documentation is a sign of weak pattern recognition and makes it harder to glean the important takeaways.

Be brutal. Simplify your message and your takeaways into what you can use. **Communicate ONLY the actionable, relevant insights.**

Speed bump #3: The false-negative pivot

Sometimes, you discover that your beloved product idea is not very compelling. That's a true negative result and reason to pivot. But watch out for the false-negative pivot. It's much easier to chase a shiny new idea than to carefully integrate feedback into your larger vision.

Don't overreact and redesign everything. Remember where you're headed. **Try tacking in a response to these winds instead of changing course altogether.**

Chapter 12

Plan Your Product Road Map

Inspiration usually comes during work, rather than before it.
Madeleine L'Engle, Author, *A Wrinkle in Time*

ALRIGHT! YOU DID IT. YOU'VE UNLOCKED THE SECRETS of driving engagement from the ground up. Here's a quick summary of what you learned.

Empathize with a Few Hot-Core Early Adopters, AKA Superfans.

Paul Buchheit says it best: ***build something a few people love, even if most people don't get it right away.***

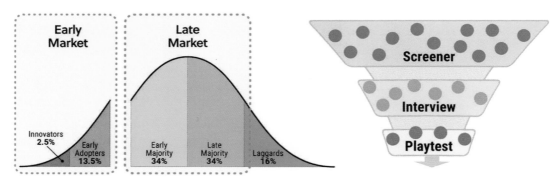

To reach the early majority, you first need to delight your early adopters. Find people with a burning need or desire for what you're building, who can help you tune your systems and validate your ideas. **Superfans are co-creators—NOT your ultimate target market.**

Create a Pleasurable, Repeatable Activity that Fits Their Existing Habits.

Once you've empathized with superfans, you use them to design your MVP or alpha around existing their habits and needs. You build a simple, compelling learning loop around your core systems and then leverage your superfans to give your feedback, validate your ideas, and bring those systems to life.

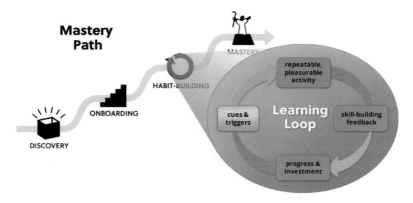

Game Thinking for Product Leadership

By now, you've heard my sob stories about what happens when you focus on onboarding without a strong habit in place. When you're bringing your idea to life, that's a perfect recipe for a leaky bucket.

You might be wondering, ***"Well, that sounds good, but how do I translate this into product management? How do I know which stage of my customer's experience to focus on during our development cycle?"***

What's the recipe for an engaging MVP or Alpha test? You can't "boil the ocean" and build out your product vision all at once. What do you build—and when?

Plan What's Next with the Game Thinking Road Map.

To answer this question, we've developed a tool called the game thinking road map. If you want to **build engagement from the ground up**, this tool shows you what stage in the mastery path to focus on, from MVP through launch and beyond.

Along the X axis, you see the four-stage mastery path that guides your customer's journey—from discovery through onboarding, habit-building, and mastery.

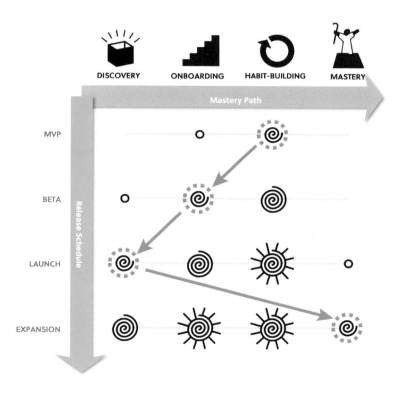

Steve Vassallo on Product Market Fit

Steve Vassallo is an early-stage investor at Foundation Capital, and the author of *The Way to Design.* He studied design thinking at Stanford and worked as a product designer at IDEO.

Early stage startups often talk about product-market fit as if it were a destination. They celebrate it like pounding a flag in the ground. "We've achieved it! Now let's focus on customer acquisition and build out our sales force."

That misses the point. The competitive landscape keeps changing. Your goal is not to achieve product market fit but to achieve a regular drumbeat of many product market fits.

Product/market fit is a liquid not a solid. Build your processes so that when you design your first product, you're beginning to collect feedback for shaping your next iteration.

The Product Creator's Journey

The stages of our journey as product creators follow the Y axis. The process starts with an MVP, prototype, or first playable; and continues through alpha, beta, launch, and expansion—because no product is truly done at launch these days.

As product creators and managers, our journey takes us from idea to launch. If you want to build an engaging product experience, emulate the teams who produced lasting hits and use this road map to guide your way.

Start by Iterating and Tuning Your Learning Loop

The purpose of an MVP is to test high-risk assumptions and understand your early market. As you know by now, ***MVP is a liquid, not a solid.***

The sooner you get started, the further you'll go and the more iterations of the build-measure-learn cycle you'll move through.

Don't kick off your project by developing a slick onboarding experience. By definition, early adopters will be comfortable using your product without a lot of hand-holding.

What's most important at this stage is to find the "hook" that can get people coming back regularly, even if it's in nascent form.

To get more from your testing sessions, do what the teams behind *Rock Band*, *The Sims*, *Covet Fashion*, Happify, and Pley did: start by iterating and refining your core learning loop.

As You Grow and Scale, Refine Onboarding

Once you've developed a strong learning loop, you're ready to support growth and scaling. To do this, you'll need *some* type of onboarding and discovery. But what type?

When starting to scale, begin with simple, low-fidelity experiments that you can learn from and iterate quickly—because at that point, learning is your primary goal. To grow further, you'll need to design an effective onboarding system, which will allow you to scale to a larger, less "insider" audience.

To build and run your beta (closed and/or open), you'll want to develop, test, and tweak your onboarding mechanics even further.

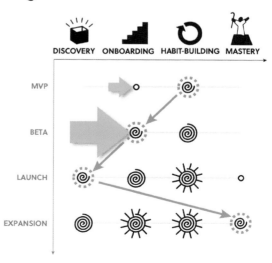

Optimize Discovery at Launch

During this growth period, you'll also develop discovery materials through outreach, advertising, and word of mouth.

At this point of the creator's journey, you're running high-learning discovery experiments and fine-tuning your targeting in order to attract the customers you want.

When you're ready to launch, all those discovery experiments pay off and come into the foreground, and you'll use the knowledge you gained to craft a compelling discovery message that reaches the right people and helps them find your product.

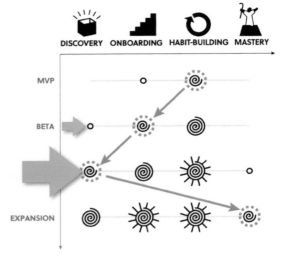

Co-Develop Your Mastery Systems with Experts

The role of mastery is an oft-misunderstood piece of this puzzle. What makes your product engaging to master? What skill is your customer building? How is progress communicated and celebrated? How does your system enable social interactions, through comparison, battles and contests? Or joining together to reach a shared goal?

If you're building a game, skill and mastery are woven into your development process. If you aspire to build a game-like system, start by identifying the skills that your players will master. Ask yourself: What can our most skilled and passionate players contribute? What enhanced role or powers could they earn as a reward for their enthusiasm?

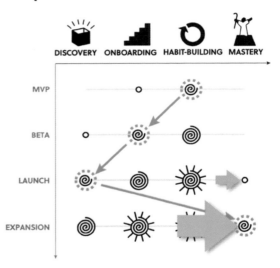

Take your cues from the habits and desires of your experts—the people who master your systems and long to go deeper. Your goal is to create systems that tap into the deep needs and motivations of your most passionate players.

Erin Hoffman-John on Changing Education

Erin Hoffman-John is a game designer and fantasy novelist with a passion for social activism and projects with a purpose. Erin is the founder and CEO of indie games studio Sense of Wonder.

In the United States, education is a factory system. You've got a teacher standing at the front of a classroom talking at the kids. The role of the teacher is custodial. Schools put as many kids as possible into a classroom. The attention is on the system itself, not the individual learner.

A game is one-on-one. All the attention is on the individual. A game can stay one step ahead of a player and offer something that responds to what the player is doing. A game can say "Hey you've been doing this series of actions. What about this other action that might be just outside of your comfort zone, but might lead you to make a leap forward?"

Games have a tremendous amount of untapped potential to change how we learn.

Worksheet: Product Roadmap

Now it's your turn. Answer these questions to imagine how your product will come to life and continue to develop through launch and beyond.

Tune Your Learning Loop During Alpha

Imagine how will you continue to iterate and refine your core learning loop.

Refine Onboarding during Beta

Imagine how you will build an effective onboarding system, which will allow you to scale to a larger, less "insider" audience.

Optimize Discovery at Launch

Imagine how new customers will first learn about and get interested in your product.

Co-Develop Mastery Systems with Experts

Imagine how your customers will continue to participate even after they have mastered your system. What will motivate your experts? How can their involvement benefit less experienced customers?

Road Map Speed Bumps

As you're planning your product road map, watch out for these common speed bumps.

Speed bump #1: Low support for iterative experiments

I'll be honest: these cutting-edge techniques require a willingness to fail fast, learn quickly, and run sometimes-messy experiments. If you're embedded in an organization that's used to waterfall-style development and product-centric MVPs, you'll get resistance.

Get your colleagues onboard early. Educate them about the advantages of lean practices and customer discovery, and bring them along for the ride. If things go well, you might even turn them into evangelists.

Speed bump #2: Over-designing mastery systems

It's easy to become entranced with designing mastery and progression systems. I've been there more times than I can count. It's one of the most engrossing and satisfying parts of game design. But if you focus on these systems too early, you're likely to end up with a mechanics-heavy experience that lacks a strong foundation.

Discipline yourself to **focus on tuning your learning loop first**. Once that's in place, you can design and test your progression systems with input from your superfans.

Speed bump #3: Listening for solutions, not problems

Beware of the temptation to implement your customers' suggestions without understanding the problem behind the idea. Sometimes, customers come up with great ideas, but they're not designers and they often ask for features that don't solve their problem in an optimal way.

Instead, **listen for the underlying problem and the need behind solution ideas.** Once you understand that, you'll be positioned to evaluate their idea, consider multiple approaches, and design a solution that's optimal for your situation and fits your existing systems.

Get Moving

Congratulations! You've come full circle. At the start, we explored what the teams who create breakthrough hits have in common. Now you know these successful entrepreneurs use an iterative, user-centered design process that's anchored by smart, focused experimentation. And you can too.

The five steps of game thinking give you an innovation tool kit for emulating success and building a compelling product.

As you get moving and use these tools, remember a few basic principles:

- **Find and leverage** your superfans first, then expand from that base.

- **Build and test your** experience from the inside out with a learning loop.

- **Tinker, prototype,** and assume your first idea might not be right.

Don't be afraid to make mistakes in your journey toward game thinking mastery. The best game and product designers know that the way to unlock your next breakthrough hit is to run experiments, make mistakes and iterate toward success. Celebrate learning about what's wrong with your idea just as much as what's right with it.

Do this, and you'll zoom past the blind spots that hold so many entrepreneurs back.

Now go out there and innovate. Here's to your success!

But wait, there's more.

 For a special surprise, visit
gamethinking.io/superfans

Glossary

Agile: characterized by the division of tasks into short phases of work and frequent reassessment and adaptation of plans. In some environments, agile methods replace high-level design with frequent redesign.

Alpha: an incomplete yet functional version of your core product experience.

Beta: a feature-complete version of your product that still needs tuning and bug-fixing.

Business model canvas: a one-page tool that clarifies the core components of your business.

Design thinking: an approach to product creation that's grounded in customer empathy, iterative prototyping, and alternating between expansion and contraction during your design process.

Design sprints: five-day group exercises that fast-track the five steps of Design Thinking.

Experience design: the practice of designing your customer's experience over time as they use your product, play your game, attend your events, etc.

Experience prototype: a rough simulation of your customer's experience over time, such as a scenario, prototype, or interactive mock-up.

First playable: the first (often crude) playable version of your game.

Game design: the art and science of creating digital, physical, and social games, which can involve designing rules, systems, UX, visuals, sound, writing, etc.

Game thinking: an approach to designing engaging products that synthesizes game design, lean/agile methods, design thinking, and systems thinking into a design system.

Habit story: a specific type of job story that is built around a relevant habit and unmet needs.

Job story: a three-part story, told from your customer's POV, that captures motivation, context, and emotion.

Lean startup: an iterative, experiment-driven approach to product development that centers around validating high-risk assumptions with high-learning experiments.

Lean UX: an approach to experience design that embraces Lean/Agile methods like sprints, MVPs and iterative experiments to create well-designed product experiences.

Learning loop: a pleasurable activity loop that helps your customers get better at something they care about.

Mastery path: the experiences your customers unlock as they get better at something.

MVP: minimum viable product, AKA the simplest thing to build that will maximize your learning. Depending on the context, you could label your alpha, beta, or even first shipped product an MVP. Your definition depends on the experiment you're running.

MVP canvas: a strategic planning tool for building the right MVP to drive engagement.

Playtest: a test where potential customers experience your product in some form and give you feedback.

Problem space: where your customers exist before they learn about your product—their rituals, habits, needs, desires, and frustrations.

Product experience: the experience your product delivers over time (vs the product itself).

Product design: all aspects of design involved in bringing a product to life—UX, visuals, features, systems, tuning plan, etc.

Prototype: an early, unrefined version of your product that's designed to gather feedback.

Scenario walk-through: visuals (video, slides, interactive mock-ups) that show your product being used over time, in the context of everyday life.

Solution space: where your product exists, apart from your customer's needs and habits. Your solution may (or may not) solve your customers' problems and/or fulfill their desires.

Speed interviews: ten-minute problem-space-screening interviews that surface relevant insights and help you identify your hot-core superfans.

Superfans: high-need, high-value early adopters who can help you bring your idea to life.

Superfan screener: a six-question survey designed to attract and identify high-need, high-value early adopters, AKA superfans.

Systems thinking: an approach to visualizing and modelling systems, where the parts are interrelated and affect each other.

Wireframes: sketches of the basic layout and functionality of a screen-based product experience.

References

 For links to these references and other resources, visit the book companion site **gamethinkingbook.io**

Alvarez, Cindy. *Lean Customer Development: Building Products Your Customers Will Buy.* "The term 'lean' originally comes from manufacturing. It stresses eliminating waste from processes and making sure the end product is something that the customer wants."

Buchheit, Paul. *Blog Post* from July 30, 2014. "Build something a few people love, even if most people don't get it right away."

Bartle, Richard. *Hearts, Clubs, Diamonds, Spades: Players Who Suit MUDs.* "Achievers are Diamonds (they're always seeking treasure); explorers are Spades (they dig around for information); socialisers are Hearts (they empathise with other players); killers are Clubs (they hit people with them)."

Christensen, Clayton. *The Innovator's Dilemma: When New Technologies Cause Great Firms to Fail.* Harvard Business Review Press, 2015. "There are times at which it is right *not* to listen to customers, right to invest in developing lower-performance products that promise lower margins, and right to aggressively pursue small, rather than substantial, markets."

Collins, Jim. *Good to Great: Why Some Companies Make the Leap...and Others Don't.* Harper Business, 2001. "All good to great companies have leaders with ferocious resolve, and almost stoic determination to do whatever needs to be done to make the company great."

Cook, Dan. *Loops and Arcs. lostgarden.com* blog post, 2012. "Since both loops and arcs can be easily nested and connected to one another, in practice you end up with chemistry-like mixtures of the two that can get a bit messy to tease apart. The simplest method of analysis is to ask What repeats and what does not?"

Cook, Dan. *Rockets, Cars and Gardens: Visualizing Waterfall, Agile and Stage Gate. lostgarden.com* blog post, 2006. "A team that learns the quirks of its customers, code, and business rapidly will often out perform teams operating without this knowledge."

Cooper, Robert. *Winning at New Products: Creating Value Through Innovation.* "Stage-Gate® has become the most widely used method for conceiving, developing, and launching new products in industry today... I hope this 5th edition sounds a wake-up call that true innovation and bold product development are with your grasp."

Csikszentmihalyi, Mihaly. *Flow: The Psychology of Optimal Experience*. Harper Perennial Modern Classics, 2008. "Most enjoyable activities are not natural; they demand an effort that initially one is reluctant to make. But once the interaction starts to provide feedback to the person's skills, it usually begins to be intrinsically rewarding."

Drucker, Peter. *The Effective Executive: The Definitive Guide to Getting the Right Things Done*. Harper Business Essentials, 2006. "Management is largely by example. Managers who can't manage themselves set the wrong example."

Fullerton, Tracy. *Game Design Workshop*. A K Peters, 2014. "The exercises contained in this book require no programming expertise or visual art skills and so release you from the intricacies of digital game production while allowing to you to learn what works and what does not work in your game system. Additionally, these exercises will teach you the most important skill in the game design: the process of prototyping, playtesting, and revising your system based on player feedback."

Hall, Erika. *Just Enough Research*. A Book Apart, 2013. "'Early adopters will put up with cost, ridicule, and friction to get their needs met."

Hall, Erika. *Conversational Design*. A Book Apart, 2018. "How do we make digital systems feel less robotic and more real? Whether you work with interface of visual design, front-end technology, or content design, learn why conversation is the best model for creating device-independent, human-centered systems."

Hoffman, Reid. *mastersofscale.com*. Podcast and web site. "It's more important to have 100 people who LOVE your product than one million who just sort of like it."

Hoffman-John, Erin (Contributor) and Robert J. Mislevy (Author), and contributors Andreas Oranje, Malcolm I. Bauer, Alina von Davier, Jiangang Hao, Seth Corrigan, Kristen DiCerbo, Michael John. *Psychometric Considerations in Game-Based Assessment*. CreateSpace, 2014. "Applying psychometric concepts to game-based assessment is not simply a matter of applying psychometric methods after-the-fact to games that have been optimized for learning and engagement, then 'figuring out how to score them.' A better design process jointly addresses the concerns of game design, instructional design, and assessment as required, so that key considerations of each perspective are taken into account from the beginning. This integrated approach encourages designers to recognized trade-offs that cut across design domains and devise solutions that balance concerns across them."

Hulick, Sam. *UserOnboard.com*. "I'm usually highly reluctant to give out my email address, but in this case it's so refreshing to not have to enter a credit card that it's actually a relief to 'only' have to enter my email address."

Isbister, Katherine. *How Games Move Us: Emotion by Design (Playful Thinking)*. The MIT Press, 2016. "People who aren't on the inside of the game world often tell me they fear that games numb players to other people, stifling empathy and creating a generation of isolated, antisocial loners. In these pages, I argue that the reverse is true."

Klein, Laura. *Build Better Products: A Modern Approach to Building Successful User-Centered Products*. Rosenfeld Media, 2016. "Better products improve the lives of the people who use them in a way that also improves the company that produces them. In other words, better products make companies more money by making their customers more satisfied."

Kelley, Tom. *The Art of Innovation: Lessons in Creativity from IDEO, America's Leading Design Firm*. Crown Business, 2001. "Fail often to succeed sooner."

Kim, Amy Jo. *Community Building on the Web: Secret Strategies for Successful Online Communities*. Peachpit Press, 2006. "Initially, it's up to you to define your purpose, choose your feature set, and set a particular tone, but as your community grows and matures, your members can and should play a progressively larger role in building and maintaining the community culture."

Kohn, Alfie. *Punished by Rewards: The Trouble with Gold Stars, Incentive Plans, A's, Praise, and Other Bribes*. Houghton Mifflin, 1999. "In fact, the more we use artificial inducements to motivate people, the more they lose interest in what we're bribing them to do. Rewards turn play into work, and work into drudgery."

Koster, Raph. *A Theory of Fun*. O'Reilly Media, 2013. "Fun is just another word for learning."

McCloud, Scott. *Understanding Comics: The Invisible Art*. William Morrow, 1994. "When we abstract an image through cartooning, we're not so much eliminating details as we are focusing on specific details. By stripping down an image to its essential 'meaning,' an artist can amplify that meaning in a way that realistic art can't."

Moore, Geoffrey. *Crossing the Chasm*. Harper Business, 2014. "Entering the mainstream market is an act of burglary, of breaking and entering, of deception, often even of stealth."

Nielsen, Jakob. *Paper Prototyping Training Video*. Nielsen Norman Group. "Convince skeptical members of your team who do not believe that it is possible to test unpolished designs; showing beats telling."

Olsen, Dan. *The Lean Product Playbook: How to Innovate with Minimum Viable Products and Rapid Customer Feedback*. Wiley, 2015. "While the first 'prototype' you test *could* be your live product, you can gain faster learning with fewer resources by testing your hypotheses *before* you build your product."

Osterwalder, Alexander and Yves Pigneur. *Business Model Generation: A Handbook for Visionaries, Game Changers, and Challengers.* Wiley, 2010. "Business Model Generation is a practical, inspiring handbook for anyone striving to improve a business model—or craft a new one."

Pink, Daniel. *Drive: The Surprising Truth About What Motivates Us*. Riverhead Books, 2011. "Control leads to compliance; autonomy leads to engagement."

Portigal, Steve. *Interviewing Users: How to Uncover Compelling Insights*. Rosenfeld Media, 2013. "Great interviewers make deliberate, specific choices about what to say, when to say it, how to say it, and when to say nothing."

Ries, Erik. T*he Lean Startup: How Today's Entrepreneurs Use Continuous Innovation to Create Radically Successful Businesses*. Random House, 2011. "To increase your chances of success, minimize your time through the build-measure-learn cycle."

Rogers, Everett. *Diffusion of Innovations*. Free Press, 2003. "Diffusion is essentially a social process through which people talking to people spread an innovation."

Ryan, Richard M. and Edward L. Deci. *Self-Determination Theory: Basic Psychological Needs in Motivation, Development, and Wellness*. The Guilford Press, 2017. "That most people show considerable effort, agency, and commitment in their lives appears, in fact, to be more normative than exceptional, suggesting some very positive and persistent features of human nature."

Schell, Jesse. *Art of Game Design: A Book of Lenses*. CRC Press, 2008. "Good game design happens when you view your game from as many perspectives as possible."

Sellers, Mike. *Advanced Game Design: A Systems Approach*. Addison-Wesley Professional, 2017. "Games seem to me to be unique in their ability to allow us to create and interact with systems, to really get to know what systems are and how they operate."

Sierra, Kathy. *Upgrade your users, not just your product*. Blog Post, 2005. "To the brain, learning new things is inherently pleasurable. So if markets are conversations, why not use the conversation to help someone learn?"

Traynor, Des, Paul Adams, Geoffrey Keating. *Intercom on Jobs-to-be-Done*. Intercom, 2016. "When you're solving needs that already exist, you don't need to convince people they need your product."

Vassallo, Steve. *The Way to Design*. Foundation Capital, 2017. "Systems thinking is a mindset—a way of seeing and talking about reality that recognizes the interrelatedness of things. Systems thinking sees collections of interdependent components as a set of relationships and consequences that are at least as important as the individual components themselves. It emphasizes the emergent properties of the whole that neither arise directly, nor are predictable, from the properties of the parts."

Wodtke, Christina. *Pencil Me In: The Business Drawing Book for People Who Can't Draw.* Boxes & Arrows, 2017. "Where are the simple books on how to draw for grown-ups? Most books that teach drawing are intimidating. They teach you how to draw buildings or race cars or realistic people, but that's not what non-designers need to draw every day. I decided to make a book for working professionals that wouldn't scare anyone away and would teach you how to draw the kinds of things you need to think through product and business decisions."

Wodtke, Christina. *Radical Focus: Achieving Your Most Important Goals with Objectives and Key Results*. Cucina Media, 2016. "One: set inspiring and measurable goals. Two: make sure you and your team are always making progress toward that desired end state. No matter how many other things are on your plate. And three: set a cadence that makes sure the group both remembers what they are trying to accomplish and holds each other accountable."

Zimmerman, Eric and Katie Salen Tekinbas. *Rules of Play: Game Design Fundamentals*. MIT Press, 2003. "We look closely at games as designed systems, discovering patterns within their complexity that bring the challenges of games design into full view."

Index

Y

Z

About the Author

Named by *Fortune* as one of the top 10 influential women in games, Amy Jo Kim is a social game designer, community architect, and startup coach. Her design credits include *Rock Band*, *The Sims*, eBay, Netflix, *Covet Fashion*, nytimes.com, Ultima Online, Happify and Pley. She pioneered the idea of applying game design to digital services, and is known for her book, *Community Building on the Web* (Peachpit, 2000). She holds a PhD in Behavioral Neuroscience from the University of Washington and a BA in Experimental Psychology. Amy Jo is passionate about helping entrepreneurs innovate faster and smarter; she teaches Game Thinking at Stanford University and is an adjunct professor of Game Design at the USC School of Cinematic Arts.

About the Illustrator

Scott Kim is a world-renowned graphic designer, puzzle designer, ambigram artist, and math educator. He developed teaching materials for the Design Thinking program at Stanford University, and educational games for ABCmouse.com. His puzzles have appeared in games like *Tetris* and *Bejeweled*, magazines like *Scientific American* and *Discover*, and books like *The Little Book of Big Mind Benders* and *The Playful Brain*. He authored the first book on ambigrams, *Inversions*, in 1981. He holds a PhD in Computers and Graphic Design, as well as a BA in Music from Stanford University. He now designs educational math games.

Printed in Great Britain
by Amazon